Women and Literature
1779–1982

Women and Literature 1779–1982:

The Collected Papers of Muriel Bradbrook
Volume 2

M. C. BRADBROOK
Professor of English Emerita,
University of Cambridge and Fellow of
Girton College

THE HARVESTER PRESS · SUSSEX
BARNES & NOBLE BOOKS · NEW JERSEY

First published in Great Britain in 1982 by
THE HARVESTER PRESS LIMITED
Publisher: John Spiers
16 Ship Street, Brighton, Sussex

and in the USA by
BARNES & NOBLE BOOKS
81 Adams Drive, Totowa, New Jersey 07512

© M. C. Bradbrook, 1982

Editor: Sue Roe

British Library Cataloguing in Publication Data

Bradbrook, M. C.
    The collected papers of Muriel Bradbrook.
    Vol. 2: Women and literature, 1779–1982
    1.   Literature, Modern – History and criticism
    – Addresses, essays, lectures
    I. Title   II. Women and literature, 1779–1982
    809'.03   PN710
    ISBN 0-7108-0401-6

Library of Congress Cataloging in Publication Data

Bradbrook, M. C. (Muriel Clara), 1909–
    Women and literature, 1779–1982.
    (The Collected papers of Muriel Bradbrook;
    v. 2)
    1. Women and literature.   I. Title.   II. Series:
    Bradbrook, M. C. (Muriel Clara), 1909–
    Collected papers of Muriel Bradbrook; v. 2.
    PN481.B65   1983   809'.89287   82–13914
    ISBN 0-389-20295-9

Photoset in 10 on 11 pt Linotron Sabon by
Rowland Phototypesetting Ltd
Bury St Edmunds, Suffolk

Printed in Great Britain by
Mansell Ltd, Witham, Essex

Contents

Foreword

'The lack of a single commitment seems to me . . . to be her rare and peculiar strength'. These are words which Muriel Bradbrook uses to characterize Barbara Bodichon, co-founder of the College which was to become Girton; but they also help to describe her own life and work. As she uses them, they are part of a defence of Barbara Bodichon against the reproach of being an 'Amateur, advanced' (p. 53)—a reproach which Muriel Bradbrook is not likely to have met with during her more than fifty years of distinguished scholarship. Yet, her long and happily continuing career shows nothing so much as a singularly fruitful lack of single-mindedness. Multiple commitments lie beneath the unique strength of her scholarship: that combination of historical sense and critical acumen, of a sharp awareness of reality and an ever-deepening sense of human personality, of which Brian Vickers writes in the Preface to the first volume of her *Collected Papers*. Multiple interests define the scope of her scholarship, demonstrated in this second volume by papers which range widely beyond the field that the world thinks of as peculiarly her own—the English Renaissance.

The papers in this volume address themselves to literature by and about women, and to lives led by women in fiction and in reality. The first part centres on the novel, the second on drama, and the third on Cambridge; and, as Muriel Bradbrook herself points out in her introductory remarks, the two essays on Virginia Woolf bind the first and third part together. What, however, is also obvious to a reader is that the entire volume—in chapters whose modes encompass autobiography and biography as well as literary criticism—is bound together by a 'rare and peculiar strength' of scholarly personality. The multiple commitments meet in a sense of wonder—the Elizabethans would have called it *admiratio*—at the symbiotic relationships of human life and literary art; and felicitous formulations convey this sense to the reader. So we learn, for example, about the Ladies of Llangollen as 'artists in living' (p. 19); about reticence in Jane Austen's later novels as 'the area where character reveals itself in style' (p. 25); about the centrality of women to the drama of the later nineteenth century, not as playwrights but as 'fertilizing men's imaginations' (p. 108); and about that generation of Girton students who, having already achieved rooms of their own, were clearly not much impressed by Virginia Woolf's talk to the Odtaa Society in October 1928, but who went on to be giants on the earth—*and*, whether poets, like Kathleen Raine, or scholars, like herself, as open to life and change in the 1970s and 80s as in the 1920s and 30s. 'So, one of the older Fellows at supper—"All these husbands!" "Only one each," I said.' (p. 122).

That little incident shows not only Muriel Bradbrook's wit—a steady delight to her listeners and readers—but also her uncanny ability (perhaps the crucial aspect of her lack of single-mindedness) to perceive similarities and differences. It is, as Aristotle says of the use of metaphor, 'the one thing that cannot be learnt from anyone else, and it is the mark of great natural ability'. The patterns of life and art never stop exciting her, and the reader is brought to share the excitement and so to see texts and contexts afresh. Most of all so, perhaps, when patterns intertwine into a nexus of ends and beginnings, as in the concurrence in Paris on December 10 and 11, 1896, of 'the theatre of the star-actor and the theatre of the poets' (p. 78): of the day of tribute for Sarah Bernhardt, showered in camellias and eulogies, and the day of the first performance of Jarry's *Ubu Roi* at the Théâtre de L'Oeuvre, attended by Yeats, a week or so before his first and most important meeting with Synge. Sometimes the patterns cut across both life, literature and criticism, as when with one illuminating stroke she relates the wives of, respectively, F. R. Leavis and Henrik Ibsen: 'Queenie brought to the partnership the kind of energy that Suzannah Ibsen gave to the great iconoclast she married' (p. 127). Sometimes they achieve the kind of cross-enlightenment which is the dream of comparative literature, as when Ibsen's Nora and Virginia Woolf's Mrs Ramsey come together as women whose 'instinct to love and cherish is in collision with brute facts' (p. 84); or when *Romola* and *Emperor and Galilean* are seen to be products of similar needs: 'unsuccessful as art', they both 'marked some kind of inner gestation that enabled the writer to move on to greater things. . . . This work was necessary to the author, and belongs to her [or his] biography' (p. 61). Some of the most exciting patterns derive from co-incidences of which the author could have had no inkling. When Ibsen was writing *A Doll's House* in the town of Amalfi, he had never heard or read of the tragic marriage, imprisonment and death of Webster's Duchess; nor could Strindberg know what associations he was one day to summon up when, in his last play, *The Great Highway*, he embodied his own and his protagonist's death-wish in the figure of a Japanese who has 'travelled, sinned and suffered by the name of Hiroshima, my native town'. But Muriel Bradbrook knows, and her readers will forever see these works in a different, more richly nuanced, context.

Of feminism as such—the aggrieved, aggressive kind—the reader will find little in this volume. The keynote, in this respect, is in the essay on 'Barbara Bodichon, George Eliot and the *Limits* [my italics] of Feminism'. Not that there is no cause: though bracketed with William Empson in the results of the Tripos examination, Muriel Bradbrook received, in 1930, a certificate 'stating that I had done all that would have entitled me, if a man, to graduate as a B.A.' (p. 113). Much later, when she had done more for her College and University than most men, a fellow committee member was to demonstrate his lack of prejudice by telling her that he 'would always prefer a first-class woman to a third-class man' (p. 121). Palpable injustices are recorded, as here, through fine ironies rather than in the strident tones of the victimized sex; nor is there any trading on the femine mystique. Indeed, this is precisely the point of the 'Notes on the Style of Mrs Woolf' which she contributed to the first issue of *Scrutiny*. Fifty years later, in her memorial account of Queenie Leavis, 'The Dynamics of Rejection', she was to look back on the group style and technique which *Scrutiny* contributors developed: 'the oblique thrust and the haughty sniff' (p. 127). But in 1931 there was something of a 'sniff' in her reference to the 'intellectual vacuum' of Virginia Woolf's 'astonishingly ingenuous heroines' and considerable 'thrust' in her claim that 'such a smoke screen of feminine charm is surely to be deprecated' (p. 156). Yet the thrust is direct and the sniff not so much haughty as concerned: what she objects to is that 'Mrs Woolf has preserved her extraordinary fineness and delicacy of perception at the cost of some cerebral etiolation' (p. 156).

The generous Introduction to the Everyman edition of *To the Lighthouse*, written forty-seven years later, does every justice to Mrs Woolf. But the concern expressed in the 1931 'Notes' points to the source of Muriel Bradbrook's 'rare and peculiar strength' as a woman, scholar and critic: her innocence of what T. S. Eliot had termed, six years before she came up to Girton, 'a dissociation of sensibility'. Nature gave her rare intelligence and the power of deep feeling, and in her professional career these have been allowed to develop in a continual interplay with profound learning.

This is why, simply by being herself, she has done more for the real

cause of feminism—as against its extreme and particular demands—
than any number of more self-conscious feminists. She knows how
much easier it is for a man to be single-minded—a female Brand is
hardly more of a possibility than a male Nora—but, as in her words
on Barbara Bodichon, she also knows the strength which comes from
seeking the truth not in an either/or but in a both/and. Generations of
her students must have learnt this; not having been among them—
except in so far as dependence on her works and, in later years, the
privilege of friendship have made me her student and disciple—I
have still always marvelled at her empathy with all those, of my own
generation, who have a double commitment, to scholarship and to
family, and who strive not to deal amateurishly with either. When
our children find in her the *livsglaede*, the energy and the repose
which their own harrassed mothers are often short on, then we look
to her as an example. The heart of the matter is, again, best expressed
by herself when (in words strangely reminiscent of the ending of
Middlemarch) she speaks of Barbara Bodichon's example as having
'changed the climate of opinion, not instantly, as did Florence
Nightingale's, but stealthily, like the influence of the weather' (p. 64).
In the same context she quotes the very moving letter which Barbara
Bodichon wrote to her cousin, Hilary Bonham Carter, in which she
sees herself travelling 'on . . . a sort of rough wooden scaffold bridge
of life, where some day I hope to see a perfect arch' (p. 64). Most of us
are still struggling along on the 'rough wooden scaffold bridge' but
doing so more manfully—not to say womanfully—for the example
of Muriel Bradbrook's 'perfect arch'. And I don't think it would be
far wrong to say that the keystone of the arch is in this volume.

Inga-Stina Ewbank
Bedford College, London
Summer, 1982

Introduction

Though without previous design, this collection seems to fall naturally into three parts. In the last quarter of the eighteenth century, women as authors began to play a leading part in the development of the novel, in which they have excelled. A century later, the image of the New Woman, symbolising a general struggle for emancipation, dominated the literary revival of the drama; although these dramas were written by men. The drama as a performing art has especially powerful social effects, not always recognised. In part III I have looked at life in Cambridge as a student of literature, and have included an article on Kathleen Raine, which has not previously appeared, and which offers a welcome opportunity to write on the first woman poet of our time; it ends with a piece on Mrs Woolf I contributed to the opening number of *Scrutiny*, and published fifty years ago, balanced by an introduction to her masterpiece, *To the Lighthouse*, written in 1978. This, I hope, binds the first and third parts together.

A similar pattern seems to me to emerge here and in the period to which most of my studies have been directed, the English Renaissance, subject of volume 1 of these papers. There was a notable encouragement of education for women in what has been termed the age of Katherine of Aragon – in the writings of Juan Luis Vives, of More and of Colet. Such learned daughters and wives of the law as the daughters of Sir Thomas More, and Sir Anthony Cooke, together with Elizabeth Tudor herself, were accomplished translators, versifiers and letter writers. Anne, Lady Bacon's translation of the chief apologia for the Elizabethan Church settlement was described by its author, Bishop Jewel, as faultless, and had been undertaken at the request of the Archbishop of Canterbury. The Countess of Pembroke's translation of the Psalms deeply influenced Donne and Herbert. In this age, translations constituted a public service by

ennobling and developing the expanding language. Religious writings, more than 40 per cent of all publications under Elizabeth (more
than 50 per cent earlier) offered women the best chance for print;
before 1500, of the only three printed works by women to appear,
two were devotional (the works of Julian of Norwich, and extracts
from Margery Kempe); and the third, if indeed by a woman, was
Juliana Berners' *Boke of Huntyng and Haukyng and also of Coota-
muris*.

From Chaucer's day, when the Royal Court settled permanently in
London the ladies of Court had commanded literature; they were
skilful recounters of stories, whether at Court or as old wives' tales,
in a culture still largely oral. However, towards the end of the
sixteenth century, the image of woman began to dominate the art of
the theatre, and also to come into print. Shakespeare, Marston,
Webster and Middleton set women at the centre of their plays, both
tragedy and comedy; Thomas Heywood constituted himself their
champion, writing a *History of Women*. These plays very often
combine the feminine with the exotic, but only rarely with the
socially innovatory. It is dangerous to become the focus and channel
for dreams.

A reformed Church (with women martyrs ranging from Anne
Askew to Lady Jane Grey) a large urban society, and a relatively high
degree of social mobility encouraged the emancipation of woman
and of her image. England was termed 'the hell of horses, purgatory
of servants and paradise of women'.

Two centuries later, the general spirit of revolution was to give
opportunity not only for social rebels but for conformists to advance.
Fanny Burney was absurdly self-effacing; Anna Seward, the Swan of
Lichfield, a friend of Dr Johnson; Maria Edgeworth termed her
works 'Moral Tales' and did not favour the term 'novel'. In the year
that Jane Austen was born, the effect of excessive novel reading upon
Miss Lydia Languish supplied the mainspring of the action in
Sheridan's comedy of life at Bath, *The Rivals* (1775). Within a few
years, however, the Ladies of Llangollen had set up their Gothic
Paradise together – today they would be proudly termed lesbians.

Jane Austen's work fully embodies the potential of her time for the
woman writer – burlesque of Gothic romance and patterns of
education for young women entering the world. The true advance of
women was disguised by protective colouring. Elizabeth Garrett, the
first woman in England to qualify in medicine, was praised by her
friend Emily Davies as a valuable ally since 'she looked exactly like
one of those girls whose instinct is to do what you tell them'.

On stage Sarah Bernhardt appeared fragile, elegant, exquisitely
refined; she became the first actress with an international circuit.

However, her repertoire was conservative and did not include any drama of the New Woman. Ibsen himself declared 'I am not a feminist'. The feminism of Shaw and Wells, like the social toughness of the romantic Alice Meynall, or the activities of Maud Gonne in Ireland, exploited literature for social ends.

The story of the twentieth century, being too complex even for a lightning sketch, is left to be seen terms of my own life, which began in the reign of Edward VII. I took my turn to push my grandmother's bathchair to the polling booth, where she recorded her first vote: 'What a pity it could not help to put in power Mr Gladstone, whom she had so much admired!'

The Novel

I.

Living the Gothic Pastoral Romance: the Ladies of Llangollen

The eighteenth century, an era of reason, politeness and limited horizons, also coined the term *enthusiast*. In literature and life it was possible still to combine the traditional and the individual, as in the work of Crabbe or of Cowper, most conservative of literary revolutionaries. The lives of the Ladies of Llangollen, Lady Eleanor Butler and Miss Sarah Ponsonby, at once daring and conventional, sociable and solitary, eccentric and polite, illustrate both the starchy independence which made an 'English Miss' the model of feminism for a whole continent, and 'that agreeable *aisance*, that air of the world of the *ancien régime*, courteous and entertaining without the slightest affectation' with which in their old age they charmed Prince Pückler-Muskau.[1]

The long lives of the ladies span their whole century.[2] Lady Eleanor was a child at the time of the 'Forty-five': Miss Ponsonby's last letter discusses the Reform Bill. From the days when they provided scandal for the local gentry to those when they stirred the easy ribaldry of Lockhart and Lady Louisa Stuart, they remained objects of interest to a vast and constantly increasing acquaintance. Letters to them survive from Burke and Canning ('his address is *Foreign Office*, for mutton as well for letters'), Wellington (who signs himself 'ever yours most affectionately, Wellington') and Wilberforce; Wordsworth wrote two poems to them[3] and Southey sent them his verses. They had been intimate with the Swan of Lichfield, Miss Anna Seward, with Miss Bowdler and Hester Lynch Piozzi; Maria Edgeworth, Hannah More and Mme de Genlis were among their correspondents and visitors. Prince Pückler-Muskau was speaking no more than truth when he described them as 'the two most celebrated virgins in Europe'.[4] But as curiosities or freaks their reputation, though great in their lifetime, must rightly have been ephemeral. They were more than this. The note of tenderness and esteem in the letters of Burke and Wilberforce, the grudging tribute of Lockhart, imply that their claims rested on genuine charm of mind and personality, and the diary of Lady Eleanor, full extracts from which have only recently been published,[5] reflects a creative peace of mind which had been fostered by years of tranquil country living in constant intercourse with books. Her epigraphs come from Gray's *Elegy* and from Marvell's *Garden*, and the serenity of the story is undisturbed by the news of war or revolution which occasionally intrudes. The ladies passed their half-century in the Vale of Llangollen in what appears to have been unbroken felicity. Their manners and outlook, formed in the 1770s, when sentiment and the cult of the Gothic ruled, grew outmoded as the years passed, even as their unvarying costume of riding-habits and beaver hats, piquant in youth, seemed by 1829 'somewhat ludicrous' even to the sympathetic observer.

The great adventure and turning-point of their lives occurred in April–May 1778. After an abortive attempt at a secret elopement, Eleanor, the daughter of Walter Butler, *de jure* 16th Earl of Ormonde – the titles lost by attainder in 1715 were restored in 1792 to her brother – and Miss Ponsonby, daughter of a cadet of the Bessboroughs and the ward of Sir William and Lady Elizabeth Fownes, set out together at six in the morning of Monday, 4 May, 'as merry as possible' in a post-chaise. This decision followed a month of tears and entreaties from female relations and Bible oaths on bended knees from gentlemen. They left Woodstock, the seat of the Fownes at Inistioge, Co. Kilkenny, Lady Eleanor having fled there from her relatives; they crossed from Waterford to Milford Haven and soon afterwards set up house at Plâs Newydd in Llangollen Vale, never to spend a night from home for the half-century of their residence. They were followed by a faithful servant, Mary Caryll, who became a great power in the household and who is buried with them at Llangollen.

It was difficult for their relatives to believe that two young women should run away without there being a gentleman in the case. 'The Family . . . imagined she was gone to marry some Body' when Lady Eleanor first was missed,[6] only to find 'there were no gentlemen concerned, nor does it appear to be anything more than a scheme of Romantic Friendship'. Nor were the ladies crossed in love as was generally thought. Lady Eleanor had 'reached the age of thirty without having one lover'.[7] She lived in a state of war with an imperious and ill-tempered mother, with the threat of a convent held over her, for the family were Catholics. Sarah Ponsonby was in a more distressing situation for she was a penniless orphan, and her guardian, Sir William Fownes, was pursuing her with most un-

welcome attentions. His 'gallantry' is hinted at in the correspondence of other ladies, but plainly shown in Sarah's, and it seems no
more than justice that, little more than a month after the elopement, this unpleasant gentleman should die of a 'gout in the
stomach'.[8]

The first clandestine flight of 2 April was indeed highly romantic.
Miss Ponsonby jumped out of a window, armed with a pistol: Lady
Eleanor was hidden at hand, both being 'in Men's Cloaths'[9] and they
spent two nights in a barn and walked over a mountain before they
were traced to Waterford by their families and brought back. But a
month of wrangling, during which Sarah fell ill – perhaps as a result
of the adventure in the barn – only confirmed their resolution. Flight
dwindled to departure by a post-chaise: perhaps to the entreaties of
their families they had replied with an ultimatum.[10] For the brute fact
was they had no money. Lady Eleanor was dependent upon her
infuriated parents, Miss Ponsonby upon distant relatives and later on
her step-brother, who was, however, at this time only fifteen.
Complete destitution was undoubtedly a possibility.

Yet, from the first, whatever their material problems might be, the
ladies proceeded, in the spirit of the Romances, to live a life of
sentiment in surroundings as Gothic as could be devised. Their
cottage was adorned in the manner of Strawberry Hill, their notion
of what constituted Gothic being quite uninfluenced by the familiar
glories of Kilkenny Castle. The plain six-roomed white cottage
disappeared beneath oak panelling conveniently supplied from
neighbouring ruins: the library was built, the garden was carefully
planned with waterfalls and grottoes and a Gothic cowshed erected
for their single cow. The visitor of today will find at Plâs Newydd a
jumble of pew-ends used as balusters, bits of rare stained glass, old
Spanish leather and above all a patchwork of old oak covering every
inch of the interior with a madly juxtaposed mass of figures, inscrip-
tions, panels and arms. The exterior has received some embellish-
ment since the ladies' time and much has been added to the older
structure, but the original porches remain. The gravel walk by the
stream with its rustic bridges and cascade seems least incrusted with
improvements of the later inhabitants. On the fountain, composed of
a font which was removed from the ruins of a neighbouring abbey, is
inscribed:

> Drink, gentle pilgrim, from the well
> Thus sacred in this hollow dell!
> Drink deep! – yet ere the yearning lip
> Touches the draught it longs to sip,
> Pray for the souls of those who gave
> This font that holds the limpid wave.

This holy font which lay o'erthrown
Mid Valle Crucis' shadows brown

And which the hands of holy men
Have blest, but ne'er can bless again.
Drink, happy pilgrim, drink and pray
At morning dawn or twilight grey, –
Pray for the souls of those who gave
This font that holds the limpid wave.
E.B   1782   S.P.

Miss Anna Seward's enthusiastic poem *Llangollen Vale*, published in 1795, works up into poetic form the impressions of a recent
visit and is the prelude to a fairly lengthy correspondence. In this
poem the ladies' happiness is favourably contrasted with the lot of
the monks of Valle Crucis Abbey under 'superstition's rod'. 'Wore
one young lip gay Eleanora's smile?' demands Miss Seward. 'Did
Zara's look serene one tedious hour beguile?' By now the ladies were
famous.[11] Miss Seward's celebrated description in its prose version
was widely known, and forty years later it is used by an auctioneer to
draw up the catalogue for the sale of the property.[12] From this
description the ladies emerge as artists in living, worthy to rank with
those contemporary writers who opened the world of letters to
women. The full splendours of Miss Seward's style are aroused by
the united charms of noble blood and Gothic taste, feminism and
sensibility, and her extensive raptures provide the most detailed
picture of the ladies to survive.

After dinner, our whole party returned to drink tea and coffee in that
retreat which breathes all the witchery of genius, taste, and sentiment.
You remember Mr Hayley's poetic compliment to the sweet miniature
painter, Miers:

His magic pencil, in its narrow space,
Pours the full portion of uninjur'd grace.

So it may be said of the talents and exertion which converted a cottage, in
two acres and a half of turnip ground, to a fairy palace, amid the bowers
of Calypso.

It consists of four small apartments: the exquisite cleanliness of the
kitchen, its utensils and its auxiliary offices vying with the finished
elegance of the gay, the lightsome little dining room, as that contrasts the
gloomy, yet superior grace of the library, into which it opens.

This room is fitted up in the Gothic style, the door and large sash
windows of that form, and the latter of painted glass 'shedding the dim
religious light'. Candles are seldom admitted into this apartment. The
ingenious friends have invented a kind of prismatic lantern, which
occupies the whole elliptic arch of the Gothic door. This lantern is of cut
glass, variously coloured, enclosing two lamps with their reflectors. The
light it imparts resembles that of a volcano, sanguine and solemn. It is

assisted by two glow-worm lamps, that, in little marble reservoirs, stand on the opposite chimney piece, and these supply the place of the here always chastised daylight, when the dusk of evening sables, or when night wholly involves the thrice-lovely solitude.

A large Aeolian harp is fixed in one of the windows, and when the weather permits them to be opened, it breathes its deep tones to the gale, swelling and softening as that rises and falls.

> Ah me! what hand can touch the strings so fine,
> Who up the lofty diapason roll
> Such sweet, such sad, such solemn airs divine,
> And let them down again into the soul!

This saloon of the Minervas contains the finest editions, superbly bound, of the best authors, in prose and verse, which the English, Italian and French languages boast, contained in neat wire cases: over them the portraits, in miniature, and some in larger ovals, of the favourite friends of these celebrated votaries to that sentiment which exalted the characters of Theseus and Perithous, of David and Jonathan.

Between the picture of Lady Bradford and the chimney piece hangs a beautiful entablature, presented to the ladies of Llangollen Vale by Madam Sillery, late Madam Genlis. It has convex miniatures of herself and her pupil Pamela; between them, pyramidically placed, a garland of flowers, copied from a nosegay, gathered by Lady Eleanor in her bowers, and presented to Madam Sillery. [From the catalogue of sale it appears that this was executed by Madame de Genlis's royal pupil, Mlle d'Orléans.]

After expatiating on the kitchen garden, the dairy, with its little machine answering the purpose of a churn which enabled the ladies to make their own butter, Miss Seward passes to the garden, the gravel walk by the brook, the seat upon the knoll with its inscription, 'O cara Selva! e Fiumicello amato!',[13] strays back to the library 'at the dusk hour' where the prismatic lantern is diffusing 'a light gloomily glaring', and looks out on the lawn, the shrubbery, the hill and the distant slopes of the mountain. She then proceeds:

You will expect that I say something of the enchantresses themselves, beneath whose plastic wand these peculiar graces arose. Lady Eleanor is of middle height, and somewhat beyond the embonpoint as to plumpness: her face round and fair, with the glow of luxuriant health. She has not fine features, but they are agreeable; enthusiasm in her eye, hilarity and benevolence in her smile. Exhaustless is her fund of historic and traditionary knowledge, and of every thing passing in the present eventful period. She has uncommon strength and fidelity of memory; and her taste for works of imagination, particularly for poetry, is very awakened, and she expresses all she feels with an ingenuous ardour, at which the cold-spirited beings stare. I am informed that both these ladies read and speak most of the modern languages. Of the Italian poets, especially of Dante, they are warm admirers.

Miss Ponsonby, somewhat taller than her friend, is neither slender nor otherwise, but very graceful. Easy, elegant, yet pensive, is her address and manner:

Her voice, like lovers watch'd, is kind and low.

A face rather long than round, a complexion clear but without bloom, with a countenance which, from its soft melancholy, has peculiar interest. If her features are not beautiful, they are very sweet and feminine. Though the pensive spirit within permits not her lovely dimples to give mirth to her smile, they increase its sweetness, and consequently her power of engaging the affections. We see, through their veil of shading reserve, that all the talents and accomplishments which enrich the mind of Lady Eleanor, exist, with equal powers, in this her charming friend.

Such are these extraordinary women, who, in the bosom of their deep retirement, are sought by the first characters of the age, both as to rank and talents. To preserve that retirement from too frequent invasion, they are obliged to be somewhat coy as to accessibility.[14]

Mme de Genlis gives a similar account of the ladies' appearance and was also much struck with the Aeolian harp, which was placed in her bedroom. She had been invited to visit them as examples of perfect friendship (*veritable amitié*), and her fancy embroidered wildly, describing them as born in the same hour, both left orphans in their infancy, and eloping together at seventeen. This information she claimed to derive from Lord Castlereagh who introduced her![15] She placed the cottage on top of a mountain, and greatly elaborated its gardens and grounds.

Such enthusiastic visitors saw little of the true life of Plâs Newydd which the ladies lived together and alone. There was a deep division between the social arts, so elegantly practised, and that inner privacy into which Lady Eleanor's diary permits a fleeting glance. The division is reflected in the style of her writings. Such letters as survive are written with the mixture of gush and circumlocution that sensibility demanded: the record of the diary is plain and transparent, built on the steady rhythm of the seasons. The first entry for each day is a note of the outlook. Some of these pictures in their felicity of detail and sober richness of phrase recall the greater diarist of the Quantocks and the Lakes, Dorothy Wordsworth.

22 November. White glittering frost. Country magnificently beautiful. A Fair in the village. What a picture might be drawn from our Parlour Window of the crowds descending from the opposite mountain and passing through the fields before our Cottage. Some on horseback, many on foot, all comfortably clad, each bringing their different commodity to the Fair as Cattle, Pigs, Poultry, eggs, cheese, Woollen cloth, Baskets, Wooden ware, Spinning wheels. The women knitting as they went along . . .

July 22nd. Rose at seven. Delicious soft grey morning . . . Rooks cawing, sheep bleating. Rush of water. Weaver's loom. Village bell tolling. Such an assembly of rural noises . . .

October 22nd.   Beauteous day. Hum of bees and insects, sweet wild notes of birds, bleating of sheep, cackling of geese, songs and whistling of farmers at their Plough. The only sounds to be heard in this lovely spot . . .

Jan. 10th 1789.   The moon steadfast over the centre of our Field attended by a few stars. What stillness in the air! Her Planet glittering in the deep blue expanse. The smoke from our Dressing Room Chimney spinning up in a thick column. The whole country covered with the purest most sparkling snow. The silence of the night interrupted by the village clock tolling nine, a dog barking at a great distance, the owl complaining. I could have staid in the field lost in admiration till morning . . .

Nov. 22nd.   The same fearful depth of snow. Intense frost. Azure sky.

Nov. 23rd.   Deep, deep and universal snow. Deeper than ever was remembered. Snowing large flakes . . .

Dec. 12th   Lovely enchanting spring day. Emerald valley, amethyst mountains. Evening fine. Bat fluttering about as in summer . . .

Dec. 22nd.   Intense frost, air so rarified that the little cracked bell of Llantysilio church was as distinctly heard at our door as the village bells. Sun rayless, white and round and not to be known except from its place in the heavens from the moon.[16]

Lady Eleanor's record of the sights and sounds is that of a countrywoman and a gardener. In her devotion to animals the first place is given to Margaret, the cow, at whose calving the whole village assembled to give advice, whilst 'the old man of Bala' effected a delivery. Secondly, there was the 'poor faithful hen' whose headless body was found under a wall, destroyed by a fitchet. 'I dare say she thought of us, perhaps called on us, but we alas, heard her not!' tragically exclaims the bereaved owner, and when the poor woman who had originally presented her brought a daughter-hen by way of consolation, 'We were grateful for the Intention, sent the hen to the farmyard but did not nor ever shall behold her as the successor of one who has left no equal!'[17]

On viewing the poor consumptive sheep in the field Lady Eleanor's heart ached. 'I wish that they could take money or that I could relieve them in their own simple way!' The parental devotion of the widowed turkey-cock is noted as an affecting instance of sensibility, though on other occasions he is a 'tyrant' and potential rivals, sent as presents, have to be killed.[18]

Towards hunting Lady Eleanor is not consistent: 'At eight Mr Lloyddes Huntsman came with a Hare from his master, probably the same poor animal who made so free with and was so welcome to our Cabbages last winter.' 'A rabbit in the shrubbery. Sent to the village for hounds to hunt. No noses. Nor indeed eyes. Could neither smell nor see the rabbit, which sat before them by the Library window.'[19]

The 'very sarcastic tongue' which had chastened Lady Eleanor's Irish connections sharpened with the years; she was quick in her reactions and could pass in a truly heroic manner from superlatives of rapture to superlatives of invective without ever stopping at the comparative. 'Our dear Barretts' became 'ungrateful, unworthy, treacherous and in every respect the reverse of what we so long thought them'.[20] Importunate or anonymous callers were sharply rebuffed: 'One gentleman, two ladies walked up the field, then Rapt at the Door and desired to see the House. Refused them with proper contempt. Creatures without names. Certainly without manners. With a consummate stock of courage.'[21]

The crime here was twofold: the creatures had not brought an introduction, or sent up their cards with compliments and a polite request to be allowed to see the place. No one met the ladies without an introduction, but they would withdraw to the 'State Bed chamber' to allow gentlefolk a view of the lower rooms. From Miss Seward it appears that the ladies were almost continuously receiving callers and 'the evenings were the only time in which from the eternal demands upon their attention, I could enjoy ... confidential conversation'.[22] Welsh parsons were not allowed to disturb their sweet retirement though honest tradespeople might be permitted to see the shrubbery. The poor neighbour, if deserving, was poulticed and cossetted; if undeserving, the ladies did not scruple to use their influence to eject him.

> Saw a family coming to occupy the Weaver's house. Enquired who they were. Blanche Moses. Not good people. Don't like such neighbours. Sent to our Landlord. He and his Daughter-in-Law, John's wife, came immediately. Said Blanche Moses and her sons should not stay there.[23]

On one occasion a 'snuffy sauntering, lazy Thatcher' provoked Lady Eleanor to say: 'Think the Thatcher horrible. Told him so. Fought him.'[24]

It is to be presumed that she did not really emulate the Irish maid, Mary Caryll, who from her prowess was known as Molly the Bruiser, but her displeasure could vent itself in extreme violence of speech as a shocked letter from Miss Seward to a parson who had been snubbed clearly implies:

> Oh, no! no! it was indeed not the answer which Lady E. Butler and her friend ought to have sent. I am sorry. I am ashamed for them. In a much greater degree I am surprised. I am sure, however, that neither Miss Ponsonby's will nor heart were in that message; but Lady E., who, when pleased, is one of the most gracious of God's creatures, under a contrary impression is extremely haughty and imperious. Her sweet amiable friend, who, when she has time, can bend or soften that impetuous

temper, knows she cannot, and therefore does not attempt to assuage its extempore sallies.

On occasions, in some degree similar, I have seen Miss Ponsonby sigh, shrug her shoulders and acquiesce. On those occasions Lady E. always involves her by the words *we* and *us*.[25]

No one can be as rude as the polite. To her noble friends Lady Eleanor wrote in polysyllables so majestic that her meaning is not easy to disentangle. When in 1822 Lord Kenyon had succeeded in obtaining an increase to their pension, the letter he received makes Miss Seward appear in comparison terse and unbending.

> January 1st. Most sincerely and most fervently do we pray that many and many happy years may dawn upon your lordship with intelligence equally gratifying to your feelings as that, with which you have honoured us by this morning's post, has been to ours. We entreat you, dear Lord Kenyon, to accept a thousand thousand thanks and to believe that, important as such an addition of income will be to our comfort – and there are circumstances which indeed make it most materially so – its value is more than doubled, in our estimation, in being endebted for it solely and entirely – as we must ever gratefully acknowledge – to the interest and friendship of a nobleman whose character conduct and principles stand so high in our esteem and respect and whose kindness has such claims upon our affection. We can only repeat our earnest hope, that our obligations may be repaid with the most abundant interest, by the amiable persons who, as we calculate, at this moment surround the best of fathers. We truly rejoice in the report you indulge us in of their good health, mingled with some fear that, if you could have accompanied it with one equally satisfactory of your own, it would not have been withheld from those to whom it would have been so infinitely acceptable.[26]

It was the hand that penned this elegant epistle which flung into the flames a letter from Lady Dungannon, causing that tremendous episode of the fire in the chimney during which 'our agony is not to be described' but which instantly brought 'Matthew Morris and his wife, Jane Fisher, Harry Morris, his daughter, the Potter's wife, her son and two daughters, Simon, Peggy's father, his wife. Everyone of these good people with a pail of Water on their head' and assembled the entire village to comfort the ladies, who, after ordering 'plentiful potations of Beer' and returning thanks to the Almighty, retired as the village clock struck two.[27]

The utmost disturbance without never marred the peace of their private life. 'A day of sweetly enjoyed retirement' notes Lady Eleanor after she had dismissed the gardener for 'Sawciness', 'being determined never while we retain our senses to be imposed on by a servant'.[28] The note re-occurs: 'A day of sweet retirement, sentiment and delight'; 'A day of sweet and silent retirement'; 'A day of sweet and delicious retirement'; 'A Silent Pensive day.'

Mme de Genlis, though charmed by Plâs Newydd, considered that in cutting themselves off from all support of family surroundings and being wholly dependent on each other, the ladies were running too grave a risk. Suppose one became ill and died, and left the other alone with the melancholy duty of interment? she demanded. The only solution which occurred to her was that the ladies should adopt a tractable and romantic orphan and educate her to be the solace of their declining years. Mme de Genlis's own orphan, Pamela, proved the unsatisfactory nature of this solution by marrying Lord Edward Fitzgerald, who is said by local tradition – most improbably – to have been sheltered by the ladies when he was a fugitive from justice.[29]

Retirement meant for the ladies a leisured but intensive cultivation of the sublime and the beautiful. Lady Eleanor read aloud from 'Poor Rousseau', the 'incomparable Richardson', perhaps even 'that detested Voltaire', whilst Sarah drew maps on vellum, and 'making a great mistake in one of the Tropics, spoil'd her morning's work', or embroidered a white satin letter-case 'with the Cyphers, etc. in gold and with a border of Shades of Blue and gold, the Quilting White Silk, the whole lined and bound with Pale Blue'.[30] Mme de Genlis observed that

> the drawing room is adorned with charming landscapes, drawn and coloured from nature by Miss Ponsonby. Lady Eleanor is a great proficient in music: and their solitary habitation is filled by embroidery by them both of wonderful execution. Miss Ponsonby, who writes the finest hand I ever saw, has copied a number of select pieces in verse and prose, which she has ornamented with vignettes and arabesques in the best taste, and which form a most valuable collection.[31]

It was Sarah who planned their Gothic interiors, who conducted ordinary correspondence, who designed intricate title-pages and borders for the diaries which Eleanor wrote in the name of both, employing an almost royal 'We'. It was Eleanor who received the Order of St Louis from the King of France, addressed their more formal correspondence to the great, and even in their declining years remained the dominant power.

Their taste for fireplaces shaped like grottoes, for 'trees of beautiful Seaweed elegantly arranged', meant that Plâs Newydd became crammed with trophies. The catalogue of sale of their household goods includes, besides such necessities as 'a Green House of great beauty ornamented with stained and painted glass', a long list of curiosities: A lock of Mary Queen of Scots' hair, a letter of Charles I written to Lady Fisher during his captivity, presentation snuff-boxes, a replica of the Warwick Vase in silver, a set of engravings executed by Princess Elizabeth for Princess Amelia, a letter from 'the present king of France' (Louis Philippe). No authentic picture of the ladies survives as they constantly refused to sit, but a little sketch drawn from memory shows them seated in the library surrounded by hour-glasses, microscopes and pet cats. (The well-known full-length 'portrait' is based upon this.) Two chocolate cups bearing their arms and views of Plâs Newydd are now in the British Museum.

Dignity and sensibility ruled their behaviour. 'The Home Circuit', which they walked in to discuss any little differences so that they might not be overheard, magniloquently disguised their 2½ acres; and the 'State Bed chamber' grandly amplified the proportion of their best bedroom. Some of their inventions sound more picturesque than comfortable.

> Rose at six. Showery all night. Heavy clouds. We shall have more rain, I fear. Got two plates of cherries, one white, the other the Orleans cherry, for breakfast. Got a bundle of Moss Rose buds. Threw them in a careless manner over the library table, which had a beautiful effect.[32]

This, one feels, cannot have been good for the table. On the other hand they would oil the parlour eating table 'with the Spinhamland recipe' and take their meals in the kitchen to let the oil soak in. Gothic disorder remained their ideal of beauty as the manners of the *ancien régime* remained their standard of behaviour. Time swept them into the nineteenth century, but they lived still in that earlier age when the Duke of Wellington appeared as 'Arthur Wesley, a charming young man, handsome, fashioned tall and elegant'.[33]

Their interest in the world was an interest in personalities: pages of the diary are devoted to the progress of George III's madness, to the personal misfortunes of the French royal family, to the heroism of Pitt and the infamy of Fox, but there is little mention of the wars, though they write to Mrs Piozzi of the 'Emperor *Apollyon's*' invasion plans with 'proper contempt'. Their own connection with the world of fashion was firmly maintained by their strategic position on the Holyhead road, and in the space of one week, 1–8 August 1821, Lady Eleanor records a present from Lady Caroline Lamb, visits from Lord Ormonde, no less than seven other Butlers, Lord Thurlow, Lord Maryborough and Lord Burguish, Prince Paul Esterhazy with his wife and secretary – introduced by a letter from the Duke of Wellington – Lord Kenyon and his three daughters, Lord Londonderry and Lord Valletort. With perhaps more fidelity than they realised the ladies were reviving the life of noble medieval anchoresses, who, in the seclusion of their little cells, were visited for advice by kings and potentates.[34]

Yet, while Miss Seward was penning her rapturous lines, there already existed in Steventon Parsonage a note-book[35] containing that memorable passage on 'the cottage in the Vale of Usk' where bloomed the sensibilities of Laura, born of an Irish father resident in Wales. Laura married the noble Edward whose boast was 'No! never shall it be said that I obliged my Father!' Elopements were the only form of marriage recognised by such refined sensibility, and a majestic indifference to wealth was supported by the habit of 'gracefully purloining' any cash that came to hand. In refusing to be reconciled to his father:

> 'Never, never Augusta will I so demean myself (said Edward). Support! What support will Laura want which she can receive from him?'
> 'Only those very insignificant ones of Victuals and Drink' (answered she).
> 'Victuals and Drink! (replied my Husband in a most nobly contemptuous Manner) and dost thou then imagine that there is no other support for an exalted mind (such as is my Laura's) than the mean and indelicate employment of Eating and Drinking?'
> 'None that I know of, so efficacious' (returned Augusta).
> 'And did you then never feel the pleasing Pangs of Love, Augusta? (replied my Edward). Does it appear impossible to your vile and corrupted Palate, to exist on Love? Can you not conceive the Luxury of living in every distress that Poverty can inflict, with the object of your tenderest affection?'[36]

'As though we cared!' was Lady Eleanor's usual comment upon news from Kilkenny; whilst it was from these despised relations, as will be seen, that she obtained an income almost exactly equal to that later posited by Miss Austen as necessary to support a gentlewoman.

These family affairs could not have been known to the world, but the romantic friendship of the ladies might well have prompted the account of Laura's connection with Sophia, whose look of soft languor was 'the Charectarestic of her Mind. – She was all sensibility and Feeling.' At first sight these two flew into each other's arms and exchanged vows of mutual friendship, instantly unfolding to each other the innermost secrets of their hearts.[37] When finally her sensibility proved fatal to Sophia, 'The Death of my Father my Mother and my Husband though almost more than my gentle Nature could support, were trifles in comparison to the misfortune I am now proceeding to relate,'[38] remarks her afflicted Laura, who herself ends her days in the romantic seclusion of a Highland cottage, upon an annuity of four hundred a year provided by the unfeeling parent of her deceased Edward.

To Catherine Morland and Isabella Thorpe descended these notions of romantic friendship, and to Mrs Dashwood and Marianne the lofty disregard of mercenary fact. They, too, considered it the mark of a low nature to allow respect for the feelings of others to repress the ardours of a generous spirit; they, too, felt it a duty to assert their scorn of their near relations.

Yet, as the century drew to a close, newer and more daring adventures dwarfed the flight from Kilkenny, and unrepressed sensibility led its votaries into more dangerous paths. The ladies would probably have echoed every word of the Reverend Richard Polwhele's denunciation of their successors in the battle for women's rights:

> See Wollstonecroft, whom no decorum checks,
> Arise, the intrepid champion of sex!
> . . . each heart-beat in the Paphian grove
> Beats quick to Imlay and Licentious love.[39]

The fashion in romantic ardour swept on to its Byronic climax; while female eccentricity produced Lady Hester Stanhope. When, in the 1820s, new pictures of the Ladies of Llangollen emerge in the letters of the time, their visitors find two old women confirmed in their oddities, with the manners of a bygone age preserved unaltered. To Lady Louisa Stuart, who had not met them, they are humbugs and their old-fashioned speech hypocrisy. To Scott's son-in-law, Lockhart, they are preposterous and their cottage a raree show. His version of their flight is, however, as wildly inaccurate as that of Mme de Genlis: even when they had grown out of fashion, the ladies attracted legendary fancy.

Lady Louisa, one of the metropolitan blue-stockings, had only reports and the sight of some of their letters to go on when she declared them to be

> The very grossest flatterers and palaverers upon earth, and keeping, as poor Edward Hamilton used to say a 'gossip shop' between England and Ireland, have contrived to learn the character and private history, the foibles and predilections of almost every individual above a cobbler in both, therefore know in exactly what key they should play to every fresh visitor.

There was nobody, she concluded, who knew the world half so well, or was so desirous to keep up a connection with it.[40]

To Charles Matthews the actor, they appeared, however odd in appearance, 'the pets, the ladies, the dear antediluvian darlings'. He longed to put Lady Eleanor under a bell-glass and bring her home to his wife. She reminded him, he added, of no one as much as a famous Polish dwarf.[41]

Lockhart, who visited them with his father-in-law in 1825, was amused, contemptuous, but ended by a half-remorseful tribute to their characters. He could not resist the power of local admiration.

We proceeded up the hill, and found everything about them and their habitation odd and extravagant beyond belief. Imagine two women, one apparently 70, the other 65 [actually 86 and 70] dressed in heavy blue riding-habits, enormous shoes, and men's hats with their petticoats so tucked up that at the first glance of them, fussing and tottering about their porch in the agony of expectation, we took them for a couple of hazy or crazy old sailors. On nearer inspection they both wear a world of brooches, rings, etc. and Lady Eleanor positively *orders* – several stars and crosses, and a red ribbon, exactly like a K.C.B. To crown all, they have crop heads, shaggy rough, bushy and as white as snow, the one with age alone, the other assisted by a sprinkling of powder. The elder lady is almost blind, and every way much decayed: the other . . . in good preservation. But who could paint the prints, the dogs, the cats, the miniatures, the cram of cabinets, clocks, glass cases, books, bijouterie, dragon-china, nodding mandarins and whirligigs of every shape and hue – the whole house outside and in (for we must see everything to the dressing closets) *covered* with carved oak, very rich and fine some of it – and the illustrated copies of Sir Walter's poems, and the joking simpering compliments about *Waverley*, and the anxiety to know who MacIvor really was, and the absolute devouring of the poor Unknown, who had to carry off, besides all the rest, one small bit of literal *butter* dug up in a Milesian stone jar lately from the bottom of some Irish bog. Great romance, i.e. absurd innocence of character, one must have looked for; but it was confounding to find this mixed up with such eager curiosity, and enormous knowledge of the tattle and scandal of the world they had so long left. Their tables were piled with newspapers from every corner of the kingdom, and they seemed to have the deaths and marriages of the antipodes at their fingers' ends. Their albums and autographs, from Louis XVIII and George IV down to magazine poets and quack doctors, are a museum . . . Peveril won't get over their final kissing match for a week. Yet it is too bad to laugh at these good old girls; they have long been the guardian angels of the village, and are worshipped by man, woman and child about them.[42]

The wheel had come full circle since the days of Miss Seward's poem, thirty years before. It was left to the sympathetic Prince Pückler-Muskau – who did not find their manners odd – to observe the concord between 'the amiable old ladies', and 'the uninterrupted natural and affectionate attention with which the younger treated her somewhat infirmer friend and anticipated all her wants. The charm of such actions lies chiefly in the manner in which they are performed – in things which appear small and 'insignificant but which are never lost upon a susceptible heart.' Wordsworth, too, saw through the oddities to the integrity that lay behind them, and his sonnet of 1824, 'To the Lady E. B. and the Hon. Miss P.', deserved a better reception than it encountered.

When Miss Ponsonby died in 1831 the furniture and library were sold, and the abrupt scattering of all that had been so carefully acquired and so proudly cherished was an index of changing taste as well as of family estrangement. In 1844 an emancipated Irishwoman of a later generation declared that 'the whole place had a vulgar commonplace appearance' and 'all that remains of the taste of the former proprietors merely proves how little was required to please fifty years ago'.[43]

Yet the ladies are still remembered in Llangollen and indeed all over North Wales: the very hat-pegs upon which the gentlemen's beaver hats once hung are pointed out with veneration. Virtually nothing of the furniture remains, but the dining-room contains a book revealing secrets which the ladies would most jealously have preserved. It is a small vellum-bound volume, 8 × 6 in, lettered on the face in black and red ink 'Accompt Book' with the dates 1791 to 1800 inclusive, and it was kept by Sarah Ponsonby. With the aid of this book, some notes on their pensions, and the details provided by their wills it is possible to see how the ladies provided themselves with 'those very insignificant supports of victuals and drink' and also the books, plants, servants and other requirements which they had no intention of renouncing. The economic foundations of their romanticism bear out the judgement of Jane Austen who left the Dashwood family to live in their cottage on a total income of £500 a year.[44]

It is well known from other works of Miss Austen that a young lady who did not receive a dowry of £10,000 was ill provided for:[45] Edward Ferrars and Miss Dashwood were not enough in love to think £350 a year would supply them with all the comforts of life, and in fact, like the Rev. Mr Norris and his lady, they could enter on their career of conjugal felicity with very little short of £1000: that was possible only in virtue of the modest needs of the cloth, for £2000 is clearly expected as the minimum annual income of a gentleman.[46]

For the first five years the Ladies of Llangollen made annual totals of their expenses – amounting in 1791 to £457 7s 0½d, rising in 1794 to £610 2s 7d. Against this they set an income of £514 9s 0d in 1791 and £545 5s 2½d in 1794. They seem to have maintained income and expenditure at something between £500 and £600 a year.

The ladies had at first a pension of £86 a year Irish (which often worked out at rather less in English) and which was paid out of the Concordatum Fund established by Charles I in 1629, and charged upon the Irish Civil List. This pension was somewhat irregularly received, and was usually in arrears. There was a 'new' pension in

1791, which may have come when the attainted Ormonde honours were restored to Lady Eleanor's brother – one of the first entries in the account book is a payment to the village bellringers for the honouring of this great occasion. Lord Mornington tried to get the arrears paid to the ladies in 1788; Lord Castlereagh wrote to the Secretary for Ireland on 14 November 1801, and sixteen years later he was still trying to get an increase; in 1822 Lord Kenyon apparently succeeded, and, after the death of Lady Eleanor, the Duke of Wellington secured a pension of £200 a year for Miss Ponsonby from the Civil List. In January 1801 they paid £10 3s 4d as '2nd instalment of the Income Tax'. The Butlers, through their agents in London, appear to have allowed Lady Eleanor about £200 a year. Miss Ponsonby, who was related to half the protestant ascendancy, was helped to a similar sum by a number of relatives – 'Chum', her step-brother, the Earl of Bessborough, Lord Fitzwilliam, and the Tighes of Rossana. An occasional entry in the account book: '4 June [1791] Miraculous intervention of Providence through a real friend of My B's . . . £200', or 'May 1st [1799] From a friend indeed!! . . . £50', a small legacy and sometimes an odd pound or two from the sale of barley, hay, potatoes or an old cow ('From David Jones Farmer for poor poor Lily . . . 10s 6d') represent the ladies' incomings, which they were sometimes obliged to swell by borrowing from 'Chum' or an obliging 'Mr Rankins' – perhaps an agent – who on several occasions advanced £100.[47]

The ladies soon discovered that 'a receipt in full is one of the greatest Luxurys of Life'.[48] The patient tradespeople of the district had to present their bills again and again, and Lady Eleanor despairingly records: 'My Heart's darling and I sat by the Kitchen fire, talking of our poverty'; 'Wrote to those civil humble Jenkins at Wrexham, enclosed them the amount of their Bill, with gratitude to that gracious Providence who inspired Chum to enable us to discharge a debt which pressed heavily on our health and disturb'd our slumbers'; 'Mr Parry of the Ship sent in his Bill previous to that most tiresome Chester fair. Wrote an excuse, having paid away all the little money we had . . . Evans of Oswestry's man came previous to this most hateful Chester fair. We had nothing to give him. Lord help us'; 'Frederick the Tallow Chandler from Wrexham came alas to no purpose. What a feeling in that Spanish proverb, Let him who fears to sleep too soundly borrow the Pillow of a Debtor.'[49]

A note of lament is often heard in the account book, particularly in the earlier pages. 'Tinker, for spoiling tea kettle . . . 1s 3d.' 'Halston gardener, with horrid melon . . . 0. 2s 6d.' 'Carter's man with cart full of disappointment . . . 0. 2s 6d.' By 1800 the entries are briefer – perhaps they were averting their eyes, for the first quarter's expenditure was £222 2s 2d, a payment on account to the grocer alone amounting to £25.

Whatever their difficulties, the ladies did not skimp themselves. They paid their gardener 9s a week (the wages of a skilled man) and gave generous 'bounty' to any servant calling with messages or presents. Money laid out on entertainment ranges from £1 10s 'expecting Mr Goddard and Lady Anne Talbot', to 2s 'eels and trout for Mrs Piozzi'. Miss Seward was entertained with two turkeys, price 10s, but a hundred oysters cost only 1s 6d. Coach hire was one of their main expenses, and they paid messengers to fetch goods from Oswestry and Wrexham, an Irish woman apparently serving as a regular post for them.

Their charity was long remembered: 'I must say, sir, after all', remarked a Welsh neighbour, Mrs Morris, 'they was very charitable and very cantankerous – they did a deal of good and never forgave an injury.'[50] Children were constantly being given shillings for walking with them on the road, going well-dressed to church, or bringing them flowers. Their offering at church – where both attended in spite of the Catholicism of Lady Eleanor's family, not to mention occasional visits from 'Monseigneur', perhaps an uncle – was usually half a guinea: they subscribed a guinea for 'flannel for the Troops' and two guineas to help the French emigrants. Gifts to beggars and blind harpers are entered in the accounts, and if they could not themselves assist the needy they were ready to write on their behalf to friends. To their servants they were generous. Mary Caryll gave little parties where the supper cost 2s and ale, rum, lemon and cards came to 8s 6d. Soon after appears, perhaps significantly, 'Thomas Jones for giving Mary an emetic . . . 4s 6d.' When she died in 1809 Mary left all she had to Sarah Ponsonby, or failing her to Lady Eleanor. The estate amounted to £500 and some Welsh property. Lady Eleanor's will, proved 11 December 1829, was sworn at under £800, but some property may have been conveyed to Sarah earlier, to whom she now bequeathed all she had. Sarah's will, proved 26 December 1831, was sworn at under £2000. Her executor was William Hamilton of Hamwood. She left two annuities of £24 each to her 'two faithful upper servants, Elizabeth and Jane Hughes', who had been in her service more than twenty years. The full £48 was to be paid to the survivor, free of all deductions. The sale of furniture and effects began on 13 August 1832 and lasted a week, realising £2013 6s 6d gross. The cottage was acquired by two friends, Miss Lolly and Miss Andrews, who tried to imitate the ladies, without much success. Their way of life had been a personal creation, the embodiment of what they truly were; as artists in living they could transmit to posterity only their memory and not their secret.

The Rylands MSS

An examination of the twenty-four letters in the John Rylands Library discloses two from Eleanor, one of which is incomplete, twenty-one from Sarah, and a note, in the third person and dated 20 July 1796, which evidently begins the acquaintance. The ladies regret that gout prevented the Piozzis from calling at Plâs Newydd, but hope 'an early retribution for their present loss, more especially as the Vale of Llangollen, which they are particularly anxious shall be beheld in a favourable light by *such* Visitants – is thought to appear to the greatest advantage in its Autumnal garb'. The subsequent letters do not give the year of writing. After a visit to Brynbella, Lady Eleanor herself writes – and her style, though equally magniloquent, has much more life than Sarah's –

> An Unwillingness to let any Wretched incoherent Griffenages Travel in Company with the so elegant and correct calligraphy of my Better half prevented me from writing at the time she did and attempting to say all of Gratitude and admiration my heart felt for the Enchantments of the day passed at Brynbella. 'Rosy hours fly fast.' Those of 9 Sept. Glided with such rapidity that I sometimes think it was all a Dream – how soon would I compose myself to sleep might I hope to have the Fairy Vision repeated.

The Piozzis' pianoforte, which like the Musgroves' harp was sent ahead when they were expected, received eloquent acknowledgment.

> Really – almost Speechless from Gratitude for the new Instance of Dearest Mr and Mrs Piozzi's kindness and attention to our Wishes, they must pardon our returning only a few words of imperfect acknowledgment – for the Truly important favour this moment received, but we trust will not deem our sense of extreme obligation either less sincere or less acute for being totally inexpressible. We should say a little of trouble to yourselves and danger to the precious little instrument – and the infinite indulgence to us – of sending it. On Horseback – down Bwlch y Rhw Gelen – a feat never attempted much less Performed before, since either Mountains or Pianofortes were in existence. But 'a little' could not do justice in the slightest degree to what we feel on the arrival of this valued Precursor of still more welcome Guests.

From the letters we learn that the ladies' copy of *Marmion* had been presented to them by the Princess of Wales, and that among Mrs Piozzi's gifts was an 'Exquisite Tripod' in which 'Pastiche Incense Powder,' supplied with it, was burned. It is, however, Mrs Piozzi herself who recounts the charming story of Mary Caryll's remarking one starry night to Miss Ponsonby, 'Ah, madam, you once showed me a fine sight in the heavens, the Belt of *O'Bryan*, but I suppose we shall see it no more now since the Union.'

Notes

1 *Letters of a German Prince* (London, 1832), I, 19–23.
2 Lady Eleanor died in 1829, aged ninety, and Miss Ponsonby in 1831, aged seventy-six, according to their tombstone at Llangollen. Contemporary estimates of Lady Eleanor tend to make her younger: Mme de Genlis described her as thirty-one in 1792.
3 By which they were affronted. His reference to their home as 'A low-roofed cot on Deva's banks' did not please, and a reference to their somewhat advanced years pleased still less. This was in 1825. De Quincey, in his *Confessions*, describes them as unconverted to Wordsworth in 1802.
4 *Letters of a German Prince.*
5 *The Hamwood Papers of the Ladies of Llangollen and Caroline Hamilton*, ed. Mrs G. H. Bell ('John Travers'), Macmillan, 1930. This embodies a selection of the material at Hamwood House, Dunboyne, Co. Meath; the originals are unfortunately not open to inspection. One volume of Lady Eleanor's diary is also in the possession of the Earl of Wicklow. Twenty-four letters to Mrs Piozzi are in the John Rylands Library (Eng. Mss. 581, 892) and others were in Broadley's collection (A. M. Broadley, *Dr Johnson and Mrs Thrale*, 1909, p. 52).
6 *Hamwood Papers*, p. 28.
7 ibid. p. 12.
8 ibid. p. 40: '6th June. Sir William told me before Mrs Tighe his illness, as I said, was his own fault that he was punish'd for ... 14th June ... having first wrote to Miss Ponsonby an account of Sir William's death.' The writer is Mrs Goddard, a family friend.
9 ibid. p. 28.
10 Sarah said 'she was her own mistress, and if any force was used to detain her she knew her own temper so well it would provoke her to an act that would give her friends more trouble than anything she had yet done.' (p. 39).
11 In 1788 they were impersonated.
12 C. Penruddocke, *The Ladies of Llangollen* (privately printed, 1897), pp. 36–8.
13 Mme de Genlis describes a 'verdant seat shaded by two poplars' – not very shady trees – 'and thither they told me they often repair in summer to read the poems of Ossian'. Miss Seward wrote a new verse for it. 'Down yon Wild Vale triumphant Deva borne/Pours the loud treasure of her foaming Urn;/Yet bears my stream, as o'er the rocks it raves,/Not Tribute but Defiance to her Waves' (Rylands MSS. 581, 22).
14 Anna Seward, *Letters* (1811), IV, 98ff.
15 *Suite de Souvenirs de Félicie L——*(Paris, 1807), pp. 187ff.
16 *Hamwood Papers*, pp. 63, 115, 141, 168, 342–3.
17 ibid. pp. 211, 157.
18 ibid. pp. 164, 114, 64.
19 ibid. pp. 57, 259.
20 ibid. p. 252.
21 ibid. p. 271.

22 *Letters*, V, 251. The date is 1799.
23 *Hamwood Papers*, p. 251. It seems that in 1805 the ladies were threatened by a projected cotton mill in the vicinity, but how the horrid design was averted is unknown. See Penruddocke, op. cit. p. 32. Miss Seward also refers in veiled but indignant terms to the affair (*Letters*, VI, 230).
24 *Hamwood Papers*, p. 143. See also p. 323 for Lady Eleanor's dislike of snuff.
25 Quoted by E. V. Lucas, *A Swan and Her Friends* (Methuen, 1907), p. 288. Mr Whalley, the recipient of this letter, had evidently borne an introduction from his brother, who under the stress of some family trouble had broken a promise to the ladies and thus incurred their anger. It appears that they afterward forgave him (Seward, *Letters*, V, 111), but Miss Seward once more impresses on the gentleman the inconvenience of so many visitors (V, 251).
26 *Fourteenth Report, Royal Historical MSS. Commission*, Appendix IV, p. 567.
27 *Hamwood Papers*, pp. 102–3.
28 ibid. p. 85.
29 Their attitude towards the rebels in Ninety-eight, as shown in the *Hamwood Papers*, is one of horror, and their correspondents in Wicklow give a vivid picture of the troubles there. 'What a mischievous madman is Lord Edward Fitzgerald!' comments Miss Seward (*Letters*, V, 108).
30 *Hamwood Papers*, p. 243.
31 *Suite de Souvenirs de Félicie L——*, op. cit.
32 *Hamwood Papers*, p. 110.
33 ibid. p. 72.
34 e.g. Loretta, Countess of Leicester (see F. M. Powicke, *The Christian Life in the Middle Ages*) or Dame Julian of Norwich.
35 Jane Austen's *Love and Freindship*, was probably written in 1790.
36 Letter 7.
37 Letter 8.
38 Letter 14.
39 Rev. Richard Polwhele, *The Unsexed Females* (1798). He praises several of the ladies' friends, but they themselves are not mentioned. 'If Seward sting with rapture every vein/And gay Piozzi sport in lighter strain/If Burney mix with sparkling humour chaste/Delicious feelings and the purest taste'.
40 *Letters of Lady Louisa Stuart*, ed. R. Brimley Johnson (1926), pp. 188ff. The date is 8 October 1821.
41 Charles Matthews, *Memoirs*, (1839), III, 150. The letter is dated from Oswestry, 4 September 1820.
42 J. G. Lockhart, *Memoirs of the Life of Sir Walter Scott* (1837), VI, 76ff. Cf. Penruddocke, op. cit. p. 16: 'Some relatives of Miss Ponsonby, who knew them when alive, always looked on them as the greatest gossips.'
43 Miss Costello, quoted by J. Hicklin, *The Ladies of Llangollen* (Chester, 1847).

44 Interest at 5 per cent on their capital of £10,000.

45 Fanny Dashwood, Augusta Hawkins and Anne Elliot had this sum; Lady Bertram had had only £7000, and was therefore 'at least £3000 short of any equitable claim' to Sir Thomas. Miss Bingley and Miss Crawford had £20,000 each; Miss Darcy and Emma Woodhouse had £30,000.

46 Colonel Brandon and Mr Bennet. Darcy with £10,000 a year is 'as good as a Lord'.

47 See Penruddocke, op. cit. pp. 30–2, which are evidently based on family papers (the author being a descendant of Sarah Ponsonby's elder step-sister). He says Lady Eleanor's pension was paid to her faithful Irish servant Mary Caryll as her trustee. For Lord Mornington's letter see *The Hamwood Papers*, p. 150; for the ladies' comments, pp. 144, 190. The account book gives particulars of payments from the family of each of the ladies.

48 *Hamwood Papers*, p. 62.

49 *Hamwood Papers*, pp. 65, 82, 136, 184.

50 Penruddocke, op. cit. p. 16.

II.

Reticence in the Later Novels of Jane Austen

Irony and Reticence

Jane Austen's effective career as an author bent on publication was crowded into the last eight years of her life – between July 1809, when she moved to a house in the village of Chawton provided by her brother Edward who had inherited a fine estate, and July 1817, when she died aged forty-two. In this period she not only revised her early novels, which both appeared within a few years, but she also began and finished *Mansfield Park* (1811–13) and *Emma* (1813–15). *Persuasion* appeared posthumously (and although 'finis' is written at the end, it was still being revised and cannot be regarded as a final version) together with the very earliest novel, *Northanger Abbey*.

In the Chawton novels, speedily written as they were, new depths and new powers of implication make them the subject of very divergent views. *Mansfield Park* has been given the full sociological treatment by Tony Tanner (Tory gentry being contrasted with city wits, and both with the humble but rising new professional group); Kingsley Amis wrote an attack on the heroine as 'a monster of complacency and pride, who under a cloak of self-abasement, dominates and gives meaning to the novel'.[1] This is, of course, Amis's own version, and requires the reader to forget a good deal of what Jane Austen actually says, but it is less unhistorical than some of the American attacks on the heroine of *Emma*,[2] which include sophisticated accretions, overlaying the tale with modern patterns of psychiatry or sociology. [These witness to the invitation to participate in a 'game' that began with the invitation by Jane to her own family. Her novels excite the kind of attention to fine detail that is usually given only to poetry. When, as a young student, I was introduced to R. W. Chambers he instantly put me through this sort of test: '"Gout and decrepitude! Poor old gentleman!" *Who* said that?']

The chief instrument of Jane Austen's style is usually taken to be irony. I want to suggest that while it is characteristic of the earlier works, an increasing reliance on reticence, replacing irony, marks her later writings. These were *written* for the public, whereas the ironies of a small in-group, such as the family, remain stronger in works originally written for the family circle: both were meant for reading aloud.

Reticence is a comparatively modern word (the *Oxford English Dictionary* gives the first citation in 1834), but it is a quality as marked in Jane Austen's life as in her writings. As a child she was described as 'a judge of character, and silent'. An anonymous lady remarked 'A wit, a delineator of character who does not talk, is terrific indeed' – Miss Austen was 'a poker of whom everyone is afraid'. Her family did not feel like this, but a certain reserve is recorded in her letters:

> I do not want people to be very agreeable, as it saves me the trouble of liking them a great deal (*Letters*, p. 43).
>
> I do not see the Miss Mapletons very often, but just as often as I like; we are very glad to meet and I do not wish to wear out our satisfaction (ibid., p. 71).

When reserve thus appears as irony it encourages readers to be ironic in their turn about Jane Austen. Reticence works otherwise: 'She could give him only a look; but it was such a look as' is not reticent at all, it is merely substituting another form of language for the spoken word; but when Fanny silently responds to the reproaches of Mrs Norris by taking up her sewing, when Captain Wentworth silently comes to Anne's rescue and takes away little Charles, there is a check on speech as clear as Anne's respectful silence before her father's taunt that she demeans herself by visiting the poor invalid, Mrs Smith:

> She left it to himself to recollect that Mrs Smith was not the only widow in Bath between thirty and forty, with little to live on, and no sir-name of dignity [although] she could have said much and longed to say a little.

The significance of reticence – the power to inhibit response, or to regulate it – is that it athletically strengthens the regulation of expression and the control of impulse. It is the area in which character reveals itself in style. And by protecting new growth of feeling, it allows for the *development* of character. Reticence in the initial stages of a relationship between two people fosters a delicate and tentative expansion of feelings and reduces conflict; it is therefore especially marked in the development of any relationship between *two* people, which takes place within a larger social setting.

The growth of love in all the last three novels is developed in this way. It is the positive element in Jane Austen's style, irony being the check. When Edward's adopted mother handed over the family estates in her lifetime, Jane, writing to their sister Cassandra of this generosity, adds she still has a competence: 'this ought to be known, that her conduct may not be overrated' (*Letters*, p. 51). No one can escape feeling the affection conveyed here, but such expressions work only inside the family; outside they would sound impertinent.

Mansfield Park

Reticence was expected of a woman, more especially of an unmarried woman, and most of all in a dependant. This attitude persisted throughout the Victorian era. A recent collection of essays on nineteenth-century women entitled *Suffer and Be Still*[3] explores the social disability of women with a deliberate lack of reticence; it brings out very clearly the disabling lack of any form of employment, which in this period was so humiliating to the woman of the middle ranks of society. Fanny Price acts as companion to her aunt (without it being actually a paid employment) while Miss Taylor in *Emma* graduates from governess to companion, and, by grace and favour, is entertained as a supernumerary member of the family; Anne in *Persuasion* is useful to her married younger sister, but not to her father or his household. Usefulness was Fanny's most cherished gratification; in her blackest moment she saw herself as an *incumbrance*. Emma partly acts as companion to her father, but it is lack of employment that makes her take Harriet's 'education' in hand. She looks forward to a spinsterhood of 'carpet work'. In such a position (as Mrs Elton makes clear) a woman was commonly expected to fall back on her 'accomplishments' for her own amusement, for she could not seek any employment outside the home.

> 'Blessed with so many resources within myself, the world was not necessary to me. I could do very well without it. To those who had no resources it was a different thing; but my resources made me quite independent.'

Half a century later, when the editor of *Macmillan's Magazine* asserted 'there is plenty of work for the ablest woman to do at home, in the parish, in literature and in self-culture', he was answered with passion by 'A Girl of the Period' writing in *The Englishwoman's Journal*:

A highly accomplished lady who had to lead a very dull life was congratu-
lated on the number of resources for amusement she possessed in herself.
She replied 'But you don't know how sick I am of my own resources.' The
truth is that no human being can go on with any interest after it is once
perceived that the knowledge acquired can be put to no use (No. 9, 1868).

These 'accomplishments', of course, were originally acquired as a
means of attracting a husband; but after marriage (as Mrs Elton
again remarked) they tended to be dropped.[4] The young woman who
had an independent fortune, as did Mary Crawford, might still, in
spite of apparent freedom, be enslaved to the social demands of the
town; but Maria Bertram had 'evident duty' 'by the rule of moral
obligation, to marry Mr Rushworth if she could' (ch. IV); and Lady
Bertram advises her niece, 'And you must be aware, Fanny, that it is
every young woman's duty to accept such a very unexceptionable
offer as this.' Lady Bertram, in this respect if no other, had set an
example to all. This was the only moral advice she ever gave her
niece.

Maria, who had secretly hoped for Mr Crawford to intervene and
approach her father for her release, on his failure to do so, was
prepared to sacrifice everything for the degree of freedom (especially
life in London society) that marriage to Rushworth could confer:

In all important preparations of the mind she was complete; being
prepared for matrimony by a hatred of home, restraint and tranquillity;
by the misery of disappointed affection and contempt of the man she was
to marry. The rest might wait.

Already, in the most poignant scene in the book, her feelings have
been given directly but with more reticence. She escapes from Mr
Rushworth's grounds and Mr Rushworth in the company of Henry,
after saying

'Yes, certainly the sun shines, and the park looks very cheerful. But
unluckily that iron gate, that ha-ha, give me a feeling of restraint and
hardship. I cannot get out, as the starling said.'
    As she spoke, and it was with expression, she walked to the gate.

The quotation from Sterne brings in a whole range of tender feeling;
but Maria as a tragic figure is not allowed any other limelight; her
very pain of rejection, too openly shown, provokes Crawford to
renew his attempts to 'make her Maria Bertram again', and so
releases feelings that neither she nor Crawford can control. Maria's
education, the dark counterpart of Fanny's, may be deduced, but it is
suppressed. At the start of the last chapter she is pointedly dismissed
by the author: 'Let other pens dwell on guilt and misery.' They may
not be dwelt on, but neither are they ignored in their effects on the
remainder of the family. 'Guilt and misery' are reflected indirectly, as

in a shadow show, through the amateur theatricals which play such an important part in the opening chapters. 'Lovers' Vows' is well designed to reflect the feelings of the women players, if it does not offer the exact series of correspondences that were suggested many years ago.[5]

Kotzebue's drama, *Das Kind der Liebe* (1790), was translated and expurgated by Mrs Inchbald, an actress and one of the radical friends of Mary Wollstonecraft and William Godwin.[6] It was produced by 1798, and therefore by 1811 might have been considered 'advanced' only in rather provincial circles. Sir Thomas, Edmund and Fanny all viewed it with horror, Fanny observing of the two heroines:

> Agatha and Amelia appeared to her in their different ways so totally improper for home representation . . . so unfit to be expressed by any woman of modesty, that she could hardly suppose her cousins could be aware of what they were engaging in.

Agatha, the poor but virtuous girl seduced by the bold, bad Baron Wildenhaim, and Amelia, his daughter by a subsequent marriage, who proposes marriage to the poor but virtuous curate, spurning her wealthy but foolish admirer, are the stock tragic and comic parts for sentimental comedy. The bold, bad Baron is converted by the discovery of his long-lost son, and, exhorted by the curate, ends by marrying Agatha. All the men's parts have 'fine ranting ground'; this is crude but thoroughly *professional* theatre (Mrs Inchabld was an actress) and tells almost exactly the story of Oscar Wilde's *A Woman of No Importance*, except that there the betrayed mother spurns the offer of marriage forced from her seducer by her son.[7] The artifice of this absurd piece of theatre both reflects and contrasts with the characters of *Mansfield Park*: the Baron combines the absolute dominance of Sir Thomas with the morals of Henry Crawford – this role is played by the ranting Mr Yates, and, as he steps into the billiard room and finds himself for the first time on any stage, Sir Thomas is confronted by this caricature of himself. Agatha, the fallen heroine, is played by Maria;[8] the earnest clergyman is eventually played by Edmund, who finds it particularly repugnant to *act* such a travesty of what he has chosen for his true role in life, but he cannot resist the chance to play lover to Mary Crawford who takes the part of the outspoken daughter. Her foolish suitor is played by the foolish suitor of Maria, Mr Rushworth. The scene where the tutor and his mistress avow their love is played by Edmund and Mary, with Fanny as an unwilling prompter and deputy.

In this play, not only is the unmarried mother an object of sentimental exploitation, but love and marriage are treated in a spirit of lofty indifference to questions of fortune and rank, and with a plethora of easy moral platitudes that parody the 'impercipient and reductive moralism, the partisanship with duty and dullness, the crass respectability' of the main plot.⁹ Mrs Norris supports the play, though in ignorance of its content. It should be noted that objections to the play, though also very little explained, involve some possibility of real violence. Sir Thomas is crossing the Atlantic in time of war; his dangers are not fictitious. Mrs Norris really thinks she might have to break his death to the family. His ship was chased by a French privateer. The family *ought* to be more worried than they are, especially his wife. This real danger adds also to the stature of William Price, who had been in action and had known shipwreck and engagements. War, however, is kept peripheral, for the main interest is in Fanny, and much of the book is told from her point of view. One of the themes, a favourite one at the time, is the effect of education: the defective education of the Miss Bertrams; Fanny's better one, schooled by adversity.

Fanny's reticence is the result both of her situation and her years. The only heroine in Jane Austen who first appears as a child, Fanny is still a very young girl, barely eighteen, just beginning to grow into prettiness, but still full of the alarms and embarrassments of youth, deeply insecure, a girl who always hesitates before opening a door, tongue-tied in the presence of Sir Thomas, humbly grateful for any chance to be of use, and constantly snubbed and rebuked by Mrs Norris. She 'suffers and is still'; and while she sees the sufferings of others, she can seldom speak of them, and, except to William and Edmund, never of her own. When Henry Crawford turned from one Bertram sister to the other,

> Fanny saw and pitied much of this in Julia; but there was no outward fellowship between them. Julia made no communications and Fanny took no liberties. They were two solitary sufferers or connected only by Fanny's consciousness.

Fanny can detect not only the suffering but the self-deception of others; and under the stress of seeing Edmund's infatuation for Miss Crawford, her own stern moral code cracks a little. She knows why he reverses his decision not to play the part of the clergyman, and it is so bitter that she feels 'If at last obliged to yield – no matter – it was all misery now.' On hearing of Maria's elopement Fanny reacts with too much feeling, as Mary Crawford with too little. At first 'she passed only from feelings of sickness to shudderings of horror . . . it appeared to her that as far as this world was concerned, the greatest blessing of everyone akin to Mrs Rushworth would be instant annihilation.' Later, however, when Edmund comes quickly to fetch her to Mansfield 'The evil which brought so much good to her! she dreaded lest she should learn to be insensible of it.'

The most extraordinary judgement of all (and surely a slip on Jane Austen's part) is Sir Thomas's on finding that Mrs Norris proposes to go away and live with Maria, 'To be relieved from her therefore was so great a felicity that had she not left bitter remembrances behind her, there might have been danger of his learning to approve the evil which produced such a good.' It is true that Sir Thomas had almost felt she was 'part of himself' – and indeed she takes over a good deal of Lady Bertram's duties – nevertheless, Fanny's youth and excessive sensibility justify such a dropping of principles in favour of comfort, where Sir Thomas could never have accepted this blot on his scutcheon even to be free from Mrs Norris.

The better consolation of gaining a true daughter of the heart in Fanny is of less explicit but more significant weight, for the surrogate relations who turn into authentic ones were traditionally familiar in the novel, especially in the rise of poor but worthy characters.

If Maria had cried, 'I can't get out', Fanny might have cried, 'I can't get in.' C. S. Lewis is not the first to accuse her of insipidity,[10] suggesting that Charlotte Brontë would have drawn her better, although of course in that case 'Sir Thomas and Lady Bertram and Mrs Norris would have been distorted from credible types of pompous dullness, lazy vapidity and vulgar egoism into fiends complete with horns, tails and rhetoric.' This ignores the fact that Fanny, while pathetic, is also, like Edmund, a comic character – worthy, but comic. To Fanny, Edmund can be playfully ironic: 'Why, indeed, Fanny, I should hope to be remembered at such a distance as the White House' by way of encouraging her. Edmund's thick-headedness, his kind-heartedness, his likeness to his father in such habits of organising and punctuality as make him pull out his watch and calculate to Miss Crawford exactly how long they have been walking, can produce the most painful of all situations for Fanny, as when with 'innocent effrontery' he suggests to her that he could teach Henry Crawford, his friend, something of wooing her:

> I wish he had known you as well as I do, Fanny. Between us I think we should have won you. My theoretical and his practical knowledge together could not have failed. He should have worked upon my plans.[11]

The authoress herself indulges in open banter of Edmund in the last chapter during his transfer of affection from Mary to Fanny:

> I purposely abstain from dates on this occasion that everyone may be at liberty to fix their own, aware that the cure of unconquerable passions and the transfer of unchanging attachments must vary very much as to time in different people.

All he needed was to learn to prefer soft light eyes to sparkling dark ones.

Fanny has more in common with Miss Harriet Smith than blue eyes and a tendency to hero-worship; she cherishes such absurd mementos of Edmund as the unfinished note beginning 'My very dear Fanny', although this also has its pathos, for she has so little in the way of possessions, that the anxious debate about how to wear her jewelry – like the later debate about the silver knife at Portsmouth – link her feelings with her privations. When she is expecting the news of Edmund's engagement, and suffering the pangs of exile from Mansfield, she is still treated with affectionate irony by the author:

> She began to feel that she had not yet gone through all the changes of opinion and sentiment which the progress of time and the variation of circumstances occasion in this world of change. The vicissitudes of the human mind had not yet been exhausted by her.[12]

Portsmouth is the world outside the security of the Park (its dockyard is as near as we get to the war). Sir Thomas sends Fanny there to educate her in the disadvantages of *not* marrying wealth. To her horror Mr Crawford pursues her, for 'I believe', comments the author, 'that there is scarcely a young lady in the United Kingdoms who would not rather put up with the misfortune of being sought out by a clever and agreeable young man than have him driven away by the vulgarity of her nearest relations.' We are assured that Fanny would have married Crawford in time if Edmund had married Crawford's sister, Mary; for she is still growing, with the excessive sensibility of the young, but with sensitiveness and insight beyond anyone else in the story. That her reticence marked no withdrawal is evident since she is a person in whom anyone who wishes can confide freely, which is one of Henry's reasons for falling in love with her: 'I could so wholly and absolutely confide in her', he told Mary, 'and that is what I want.'

Trust is the basis of this kind of love; it is quite likely, as R. W. Chapman remarks, that Jane Austen could have told us where Henry kept his mistress – perhaps some little actress from the public stage! After the play-acting is over, he finds Fanny reading Shakespeare to Lady Bertram, picks up the volume, and takes *all* the parts – the play is *Henry VIII*, a leading part for which in one respect he was probably well equipped.

Fanny instinctively knows this, but her tactful – though unnoticed – suggestion to Edmund that he had been trifling with Julia's feelings as well as Maria's is lost. Similarly, her fears for Maria, as she prepares to escape from the Park with Henry, are given only indirectly, in terms which cannot offend:

> 'You will hurt yourself, Miss Bertram,' Fanny cried. 'You will certainly hurt yourself against the spikes – you will tear your gown – you will be in danger of slipping into the ha-ha. You had better not go.'

She warned Edmund against discussing too freely with herself the lady who might be his future wife, only to be assured that he never loved blindly. In a later letter he rejoices to Fanny that both he and Miss Crawford can confide in her. Later, after revealing his disappointment in that quarter, he adds

> 'I thank you Fanny, for your patience. This is the greatest comfort and now we will have done.'
> And such was Fanny's dependence on his words that for five minutes she thought they *had* done. Then it all came on again.

She finds at Portsmouth that her parents are alien to her, but when she inadvertently speaks of going 'home' to Mansfield Park, she is afraid of having wounded them. They do not even notice the phrase, and would not care if they did; 'she was as welcome to wish herself there as to be there'.

The moral views of Lieutenant Price are expressed in naval language as violent – and over-expressed (in a different sort) – as Fanny's own towards Maria: '"By God, if she belonged to me, I'd give her the rope's end as long as I could stand over her."' Fanny's inward condemnation of her mother ruthlessly exposes the crippling effects of poverty, for in effect she is condemning the qualities of her best-loved aunt and surrogate mother, Lady Bertram, whose likeness to her sister is plain.[13]

> She could and did feel that her mother was a partial ill-judging parent, a dawdle, a slattern, who neither taught nor restrained her children, whose house was the scene of mismanagement and discomfort from beginning to end.

Fanny goes so far as to speculate whether, if she were to marry Crawford, he would give a home to Susan, the younger sister for whose sake she will even bravely venture to spend money and join a circulating library, and for whose education she begins to employ her own resources of knowledge, as Edmund, her best tutor, had done for her. Not only an inveterate reader of biographies and poetry, Fanny is also a budding Romantic and her least reticent moment comes in her enthusiastic outburst to Edmund on the beauties of the moonlight view of the Park (whilst she is hoping to keep him away from music and Miss Crawford):

'Here's harmony!' she said, 'Here's repose! Here's what may leave all music behind and what poetry only can attempt to describe! Here's what may tranquillize every care and lift the heart to rapture! When I look out on such a night as this, I feel as if there could be neither wickedness nor sorrow in the world!'

'In such a night' Fanny is at Belmont (music and all) in this moment. When, on her return from Portsmouth, Lady Bertram comes eagerly forward and falls on her neck saying 'Dear Fanny! now I shall be comfortable!' Fanny receives the greeting she had vainly expected from her natural mother. She has 'got in' at last.

'They had all been solitary, helpless and forlorn alike', but Fanny and Edmund restore what Miss Lascelles has termed 'the grave implications of human interdependence numbly unrealized' in the family life of the Park. This is the essential ending of the story; though Jane Austen stretches her vista out and gives the future in perspective, she does not stay within the narrative, but gradually withdraws. An explicit love scene between Fanny and Edmund is not called for; the slow delicate growth of Fanny's maturity is fulfilled. But for Edmund, no one remembers that after chapter XXXIV he is the Rev. Edmund Bertram (though Miss Crawford's injudicious conversation becomes much more of an insult if delivered to the cloth).[14] He is in no hurry to go and reside at Thornton Lacey; he stays at Mansfield all through the summer, though ordained at Christmas. He still has much to learn.

> Jane Austen is thus a mistress of much deeper emotion than appears on the surface. She stimulates us to supply what is not there. What she offers is apparently a trifle, yet is composed of something that expands in the reader's mind and endows with the most enduring form of life scenes which are outwardly trivial ... Here is nothing out of the way; it is midday in Northamptonshire; a dull young man is talking to rather a weakly young woman on the stairs as they go up to dress for dinner, with housemaids passing. But from triviality, from commonplace, their words suddenly become full of meaning and the moment for both one of the most memorable in their lives. It fills itself, it shines, it glows; it hangs before us, deep, trembling, serene, for a second; next the housemaid passes, and this drop, in which all the happiness of life has collected, gently subsides again to become part of the ebb and flow of ordinary existence. (Virginia Woolf, *The Common Reader* (1925), pp. 174, 178)

This beginning of the love story shows Edmund discussing Mary with Fanny; his depth of confidence shows through the confession, so that Fanny with less hesitation than, in a like situation, Emma Woodhouse betrays, can, after cautioning him, say: '"I cannot be afraid of hearing anything you wish to say. Do not check yourself. Tell me whatever you like."' From little Miss Muchafraid this is indeed significant of where her fortitude lay.[15] When, after Edmund had hoped for friendship between 'the two dearest objects I have on earth', she felt it 'a stab', yet

> It was her intention, as she felt it to be her duty, to try to overcome all that was excessive, all that bordered on selfishness, in her affection for Edmund. To call or to fancy it a loss, a disappointment, would be presumption . . . To think of him as Miss Crawford might do . . . insanity . . . why did such an idea occur to her even enough to be reprobated and forbidden? It ought not to have touched on the confines of her imagination.

This is not just an application of those principles which Mrs Rushworth and Mrs Norris apply to the eligibility of Henry Crawford (What is his fortune? £4000 a year) it is the indoctrination wrought by such occasions as that when Tom Bertram, having told her he does not want to dance, seizes her with reproaches and leads her off to escape his aunt's plan for setting him down at cards.

The final test of control bred from reticence is Fanny's ability to deny to Sir Thomas that her refusal of Henry Crawford is because 'your affections' are engaged, as he implied; and saw her lips form into a *no*, though the sound was inarticulate. He 'chooses to appear satisfied', but quickly probes into her feelings for Tom and Edmund. Fanny is able, calmly and gently, to agree that Edmund is likely to marry soon, that he has seen a woman he could care for; Sir Thomas is reassured that Mrs Norris was right in thinking a common household life would be the best insurance against love between the cousins.

In 1974 R. F. Brissenden of Canberra applied a modern turn to this story by suggesting that the motif of incest gave what he considered an inexplicable power which the work appeared to generate, and that it was highlighted by the amateur theatricals.[16] Fanny, in short, marries her adoptive brother, and this is termed incestuous.

Discrimination between what incest means and what it does not is clear enough. Jane Austen, as a country parson's daughter, must have met cases of incest, even though the celebrated scandal of Lord Byron and his half-sister did not break until after the novel's publication. Two of her brothers married adoptive daughters of her own house, the Lloyd sisters, with whom they (the ladies of the Austen household) had lived. The true fraternal relationship is given a tender disquisition, *à propos* of Fanny and William: 'Children of the same family, the same blood, with the same first associations and habits, have some means of enjoyment in their power which no subsequent connections can supply.' Although such early attachments are often outlived, 'fraternal love, sometimes almost every-thing, is at other times worse than nothing'.

The delicate gradations of feeling between Fanny and William, Henry and Mary, Edmund and his sisters, Edmund and Fanny are carefully indicated. On the way to Sotherton, pointing out the features of her future estate, Maria observes, 'I am glad the church is not so close to the Great House as often happens in old places . . . There is the parsonage; a tidy looking house and I understand the clergyman and his wife are very decent people.' From the sister of one (future) cleric to the sister-in-law and guest of another, this is pretty damning.

Reticence over the end of Maria's marriage is very nearly com-plete, but this is the one case where Jane Austen shows such a collapse. There are many unsuccessful marriages – intelligent men married to stupid women, stupid men married to intelligent women. The story of Maria, sympathetically suggested, reverses the relation of her own father and mother. The writer who could give to Lady Bertram, on the news of Fanny's marriage prospects, the astonishing collocation of ideas: '"And I tell you what, Fanny – which is more than I did for Maria – next time pug has a litter, you shall have a puppy"' had little to learn from modern Freudians.

Fanny succeeded to the duties and occupied the residence of Aunt Norris, her former tyrant. She crossed the Park to the Rectory. The celebrated authorial intrusion which banishes Maria – 'Let other pens dwell on guilt and misery' – is a reminder that the story is only a story. Bereavement is another subject that is denied direct treatment, although it is important in *Sense and Sensibility*, and in *Persuasion*: the actual deaths are outside the story. The three things that Sweeney thought were all life contained – birth, and copulation, and death – are delicately reflected – in the last two novels we meet children.

Emma

We see the courtship of Fanny and Edmund through a diminishing perspective – Edmund still has so much to learn, and is almost as conservative as Fanny. But Emma receives a set proposal, although at its climax the author's reticence paradoxically intrudes to mask the scene.

> She spoke then, on being so entreated. What did she say? – Just what she ought, of course. A lady always does – She said enough to show there need not be despair and to invite him to say more of himself.

Some have been indignant at the elimination.[17] Emma who once before had certainly said what she ought *not*, and been told of it by Mr Knightley, is now only afraid of being awakened from 'the happiest dream', but taking instant appraisal of her own advantage, draws out his confession and delays her own, recognising moreover that on her side a certain reticence will have to remain, to protect the secret of her little victim, Harriet – this in itself was a notable advance on her own and others' recent behaviour.[18] 'Seldom, very seldom does complete truth belong to any human disclosure; seldom can it happen that something is not a little disguised or a little mistaken'. Yet Emma had the desire to be a clear glass of truth to Mr Knightley, was prepared when she thought him alone to be concerned to tell him exactly what she thought; and when at last Jane Fairfax reveals the plans for an early marriage, she cries out 'Thank you, thank you – This is just what I wanted to be assured of – Oh! if you knew how much I love everything that is decided and open!'. Yet again she had blushed when Knightley appealed confidentially to her 'My Emma, does not everything serve to prove more and more the beauty of truth and sincerity in all our dealings with one another?'

The decided and open quality, the plain, downright and rather commanding tones of Mr Knightley always subdue Emma, yet she enjoys sparring with him, and expects his criticisms: 'We always say what we like to each other', she tells her father in the opening chapter, and 'Mr Knightley loves to find fault with me.' But, 'I love an open temper' he had also said, and held lack of openness against Jane Fairfax, as well as Frank; whom he expected, to Emma's amusement, to be able to stand up to his adopted parents and make a protest 'loudly and standing in the middle of the room'.

Emma's brave decision to hear what Mr Knightley had to say and advise him 'as a friend' marks her coming of age as a counsellor;[19] but it could imply that when she had to find words at last to meet his proposal, she could not really recall what was said and her reply came as an instinctive and not fully conscious response. 'The elimination' might not unfairly be read as suggesting an extraordinary state of consciousness; for so much of the novel has been concerned with Emma's point of view, and the shift from an exterior to an interior view of the heroine has been noted as one of its main structural devices. Emma is on-stage in every scene of the novel except that early discussion between Mrs Weston and Mr Knightley, of which she is the subject.

Structurally, therefore, this novel is even more fully based on its heroine, but, at the same time, her degree of insight or deception and the degree to which information is accessible or withheld from her is also part of the structure.

Reticence or frankness, malice or candour, on the part of the characters builds up a plot which is buttressed by irony and implication on the part of the author. It has often been observed that a knowledge of the secret engagement adds to the interest of the reading; illusion and delusion, simulation and dissimulation run along the network of connections between all the characters. Everyone is connected with all the rest, but not always in a way that is apparent; many of the characters reflect each other, or form part of a sub-system of relations. Reticence is the positive form, as compared with irony – itself an extreme form of reticence.

The characters may be variously grouped: there are the teachers – from old-fashioned Mrs Goddard, through Jane Fairfax, destined for 'the governess trade', and Mrs Weston, who is very conscious that she started there, through Emma, the amateur educator of Harriet, to Mr Knightley, who behaves towards Emma like a tutor. There is the social scale, ranging from Harriet 'the illegitimate daughter of nobody knows who', through Jane, well-born, but poor and portionless, 'the charming Augusta Hawkins' and Emma, acknowledged queen of Highbury, up to the invisible Mrs Churchill, herself a nobody who had married so high that she becomes a caricature of Emma's worst qualities. This demon figure, whose death releases Jane from her destined fate, leading thereby to all other *éclaircissements*, belongs to a higher group than even the mistress of Donwell; though when it is suggested to Emma that Mr Knightley might marry Jane, in one of her crudest and frankest admissions to herself, she recoils from 'a Mrs Knightley for them all to give way to' (p. 228). Jane herself is kept a silent figure, a mere postulated character, who has to act a part but who, unlike Frank Churchill, does not enjoy it. None the less,

> The world of *Emma* is binary. Around the visible star, Emma herself, circles an invisible planet whose presence and orbit we can gauge only by measuring the perturbations in the world we can see. Thus, the tensions that build and break in the expedition to Box Hill are felt by all, but understood only by Jane Fairfax and Frank Churchill. The written novel contains its unwritten twin whose shape is known only by the shadow it casts. (W. J. Harvey, 'The Plot of *Emma*', in *Essays and Criticism*, xvii, 1967)

Jane Austen was accused of ignorance of the passions; after reading this novel Charlotte Brontë asserted that Jane Austen studies what she sees keenly, speaks aptly, moves flexibly, ignoring the heart, 'the unseen seat of life and the sentient target of death. Even to the feelings she accords no more than an occasional graceful but distant recognition.' Is it then a coincidence that at the moment when the invisible planet comes into the light we have two reminiscences of

Romeo and Juliet? One is Emma's excuse of Jane's deception in contracting a secret engagement: 'If ever a woman can be excused for thinking only of herself, it is in a situation like Jane Fairfax's – Of such, one may almost say "the world is not theirs, nor the world's law"' (Romeo's words to the wretched apothecary). The other reminiscence is Frank's enthusiastic outburst of how he means to have some of his aunt's jewels set for an ornament for Jane's head ('"Will it not be beautiful in her dark hair?"') Here the darkness and the jewel suggest Romeo's praise of his love. Frank's long letter suggests how expansive the secret correspondence might have been – he is certainly fluent, as Knightley observes. We never see these two lovers alone, though their public quarrels are agonising. Only once does Emma get a glimpse into Jane's misery, when she flees from Mrs Elton at Donwell and walks home – '"O Miss Woodhouse, the comfort of being sometimes alone!"' (p. 363) seemed to burst from an overcharged heart. Thereby missing Churchill, Jane throws him into a fearful fit of frustration. As we learn later, he has been forbidden to walk home with her when he encountered her on the way, so that in a petulant mood he plans a Byronic tour abroad to Switzerland with the cool assumption that he can carry his adoptive family with him if he chooses.

Next day he conducts a second quarrel in public, wildly if obliquely attacking Jane; at once the soldier's daughter, steady as a rock under this onslaught, resolute in her hard decision, she acts. Her act, which we learn only from Frank's letter, releases the springs of intrigue, coinciding as it luckily does with the death of Mrs Churchill.

The scene throughout is Highbury; no novel is more constricted in its setting. As for Emma, she is seldom more than two hours from home; even Mr Knightley comments on the fact that she has never been away from Hartfield. In spite of her sovereign rule over her tiny circle, it is that circle alone which she knows. Like Fanny she will not move, though unlike Fanny she is ostensibly at liberty to do so. This is where the utter powerlessness of Mr Woodhouse turns into a tyranny almost equalling Mrs Churchill's. He does not wish to move at all, and in spite of her position as mistress of the house and her independence of all restraints, Emma is imprisoned by her devotion to her father. Emma knew she was lucky to be 'so always first and always right' and could not hope to be so in any other man's eyes than her father's (p. 84), so she is resolved on a single life. Even after she realises it is equally important to be first with Mr Knightley, first in interest and affection (p. 415) she can only hope that he too will remain single all his life: 'Let him but continue the same Mr Knightley to her and to her father.' Marriage would not do for her because she could not leave her father; and she would not marry even if she were asked by Mr Knightley. To this resolution she adheres: 'She even wept over the idea of leaving Mr Woodhouse, as if it were a sin.' It is Mr Woodhouse who, at the end, appreciates the physical attraction of a son-in-law who can defend his house from marauders, and it is Mr Knightley who shifts his home from his beloved Donwell, to join the Hartfield tea-table and the nightly gruel sessions.

This very small circle means, however, that relations can develop half-consciously. '"Whom are you going to dance with?"' asks Mr Knightley. Emma, after a slight hesitation, answers '"With you, if you will ask me"', and, observes Virginia Woolf, she has said enough. On other occasions a smile, a glance, a hand clasp (he took her hand – whether she had not herself made the first motion she could not say – she might perhaps have rather offered it) attests how much communication between these two goes on half aware. The very fact that after the engagement Emma cannot call him 'George' but prefers 'Mr Knightley' is an indication that should not be read amiss – this is how wives were accustomed to speak of and to a husband. It is a kind of reticence which does not imply shyness, but a sort of singleness in Mr Knightley. He only has *one name*. Emma has, as it were, skipped the 'smiles and blushes rising in importance, with consciousness and agitation richly scattered' that accompanied the whirlwind courtship of 'Mr E.' and 'the charming Augusta Hawkins'. The lady is in one sense not very ready to have him, because she has already so much more than she knows.[20] The threshold of consciousness is lowered abruptly at Harriet's confession that she thinks Mr Knightley may have an inclination for *her*. 'It darted through [Emma] with the speed of an arrow that Mr Knightley must marry nobody but herself.' Only the possibility of being supplanted enlightens her, otherwise in the moment of accepting his hand for the dance she can say, '"We are not really so much brother and sister as to make it at all improper"'. His emphatic '"No, indeed!"' may record an unconscious chagrin, for he advances faster through jealousy than she. Looking at the pleasant prospect of Donwell her only reflection was that 'Isabella had connected herself unexceptionably'. Mr Knightley can also make use of his brother, however, declaring '"John loves Emma with a reasonable and therefore not a blind affection"'.

The Knightley brothers practise an English reticence with each other – '"How d'ye do, George?"' and '"John, how are you?"' burying under a calm that seemed all but indifference the real attachment that would have led either of them to do anything for the good of the other. Emma practises a more social form of reticence – thus, when Mr Weston insists on inviting the odious Mrs Elton to join the party because numbers are an advantage 'Emma denied of it aloud, and agreed to none of it in private.'

Later, when Mrs Elton conjectures where Mr Knightley can be and why he is so inattentive to Mr E., 'Emma amused herself by protesting it was all very extraordinary indeed and that she had not a syllable to say for him.' There is another authorial expansion of the dialogue which is not due to the characters at all, but depends on their self-betrayal. When Mr Weston comes to Emma with some news which his wife will break to her –

> 'Break to me!' cried Emma, standing still with terror. 'Good God! . . . Something has happened in Brunswick Square . . . Consider how many of my dearest friends are now in Brunswick Square . . . Good Heavens! what can be *broke* to me that does not relate to one of that family?'

and he assures her ' "Upon my honour . . . it is not in the smallest degree connected with any human being of the name of Knightley." ' Emma has alluded to her sister's family as 'my dearest friends', but Mr Knightley is there too. And the reader feels that the extreme terror is related to him, and that Mr Weston's choice of phrase is singularly apt as it covers everybody. The *sub voce* conversation can just be heard, as when wires are crossed on the telephone.

Emma is still in many ways the village maiden, and the fantasy she makes up about Miss Fairfax and Mr Dixon is almost on a par with the Gothick imagination of Catherine Morland. She expects a girl to love the man who rescues her from drowning, or from being frightened by gypsies, but Jane loves gaiety, her future is so black. The real stability of this little world can allow an implied code of worldliness in all the inhabitants. The admirable Mrs Weston, ex-governess, can say when her step-son offers to marry Jane Fairfax, 'It is not a connection to gratify'; and though Emma is furious at Mrs Elton being surprised to find that the woman who brought her up is a lady, she herself, when Harriet's teacher, Miss Nashe boasts of a sister who married a linen draper, observes 'one would be sorry to see greater pride or refinement in the teacher of a school'. Already Miss Hannah More and her four sisters, the Bristol schoolmarms, were moving in circles much higher than that of Hartfield. Emma's views are old-fashioned, and her imagination is not restricted by decorum; when Mr Knightley hints at his agitating news (of Harriet's engagement) she reflects that the death of Mrs Churchill may have revealed 'half a dozen natural children perhaps and poor Frank cut off!'.

Frank had been in the situation of Miss Austen's own brother, Edward. He too had been adopted by his rich relations, taken away from home, given the name of *Knight*. This echo of the situation, which had in fact brought the Austen ladies to Chawton and affluence, is only one of those hidden 'games' with family events that can be detected in the novels. It is rather like the alphabet game that is played by Frank and Jane at the party, although the undercurrents here are really dangerous. On the contrary, in that last scene in the shrubbery, where the other pair of lovers seem to be walking away into life together, emotional fulfilment is based upon a trust that in spite of misunderstandings had never been shaken. It is less passionate but more secure.

Mr Knightley, like Mirabell in Congreve's play, had dwelt on the heroine's faults so long (he had early run over them to Mrs Weston), till

> I like her with all her faults; nay, like her for her faults . . . I studied 'em and got 'em by rote . . . I used myself so to think of them that at length . . . they gave me every hour less and less disturbance . . . they are now grown to me as familiar as my own frailties; and in all probability in a little time I shall like 'em as well. (*The Way of the World*, I, iii)

At the end the authoress herself re-enters to make fun of the impeccable Mr Knightley. He found Emma seeming distressed – Churchill was a villain; he found her feelings not engaged, and Churchill became redeemable. 'She was his own Emma by hand and word' when they returned, 'and if he could have thought of Frank Churchill then, he might have thought him a very good sort of fellow'.

However, Mr Knightley's imagination first detected the relationship of Frank Churchill and Jane Fairfax; he shares Emma's imaginative world, as she shares his world of reason and good sense.

What George Eliot termed 'the primitive fellowship of kindred' is completed by Isabella, the elder sister, sympathetic and simple-minded like her father, but ready to walk through snow in her evening shoes to reach her children.

> 'I am not at all afraid. I should not mind walking half the way. I could change my shoes, you know, the moment I got home; and it is not the sort of thing that gives me cold.'

(For which her husband mocks her.) The Knightley brothers compare the handwriting of the two sisters; when John says they are much alike, George replies hesitantly ' "I know what you mean – but Emma's is the stronger." ' Isabella's considerable brood (Henry, John, Bella, George and Emma) are named after the older generation, so already the family is seen extended, as other families in Jane Austen are not. Emma, like Isabella, and like Harriet, is to be guided and protected but she has already guided her foolish old father who, as Sir Walter Scott observed, is intellectually on a par with Miss Bates. 'It is not a connection to gratify', in that respect. But Mr

Knightley who had sent his last sack of cooking apples to Miss Bates and who, if he wanted to drown her chatter would simply have raised his voice a little, by his choice had taken the surest way, unconsciously, of both gratifying and humbling Emma. The word she uses is 'sacrifice'; Mrs Weston thinks, who else could bear with Mr Woodhouse? but in the end comes round to thinking it 'no sacrifice worth the mentioning'. Mr Woodhouse in turn, whose views on marriage have been as persistent as Mrs Bennett's views on entails (and about as logical), is converted by the very mildest threat of violence that can ever have dislodged a prejudice of such long standing.

Of course the Freudians have been at work on this book, too. Emma is in love with her father – or else Emma is a lesbian in love with Harriet.[21] (Against the last, Emma's constant search for a husband for Harriet might have acted as sufficient safeguard.)

Mr Knightley, surrounded and supported by such worthies as William Larkins and Robert Martin, is rooted in the countryside; and even his brother loves to discuss details of working the land. Though a gentleman, Mr Knightley would be perfectly capable of giving a hand with the hay, and in this direct contact and knowledge of active physical work he is joined with the sailors, the profession which Jane Austen knew best. This practical employment distinguishes them from the 'fine gentlemen'; in the next and last novel we meet the most deplorable specimens of that breed.

Though here we are in the town, the country is just beyond its confines; the country and town mingle. The world seems at peace; even dependants are well cared for, and nowhere is found the chill that has to be dispelled from Mansfield Park.

Persuasion

Persuasion might be termed a study in reticence; it is also an idyll, not of the growth, but the revival of love. An eight-year-old break in an engagement keeps Anne and Captain Wentworth apart, yet for her part consciously faithful; for his part unconsciously so. Worldly counsels of prudence had persuaded Anne to think it her duty to dissolve the union. At their first meeting 'a thousand feelings rushed on Anne, of which this was the most consoling, that it would soon be over'. His first silent gesture of concern for her leaves her unable to thank him although she was 'ashamed of herself, quite ashamed, of being so nervous, so overcome by a trifle'; his second act of such a kind left her in a state where her replies to the conversation of others 'were at first unconsciously given'. The physical sensitiveness to a presence, the instinctive, unspoken bond that gradually asserts itself between them, is for Anne a matter of sensation. This is love from the woman's point of view, but known and recognised by her from the beginning as an inward response to be stifled or contained.

Both more vulnerable and more assured than her predecessors, Fanny or Jane Fairfax, Anne is ten years older than Fanny but even more lonely and neglected. No one in her own family considers her, everyone makes use of her, she is expected to sit at the piano and play dances for the flirtatious Musgrove girls. However, she has a rank in general society, and a certain confidence in herself. She knows she has been 'blighted' – the phrase was current throughout the nineteenth century – but when she meets Commander Benwick, who has also been blighted by the death of his fiancée, she gives some fairly robust counsel, advising him to leave poetry and read more moral and improving works as the best means of fortitude against affliction. At the same time she is prepared to laugh at herself because of the gap between her advice and her own conduct – such mockery was previously left to the author.

It is enough for Anne, when much later she and Wentworth meet to discuss Benwick's new engagement to the girl with whom Wentworth himself had been flirting, to hear by way of recantation from him '"A man does not recover from devotion of the heart to such a woman. He ought not – he does not."' She can interpret the broken sentences, the 'half-averted eyes and more than half-averted glances' although the 'happiness of such misery or the misery of such happiness' in a purely social setting leaves much to chance, till gradually every old and new misconception is removed. An over-heard conversation (balancing the misery of one earlier overheard by Anne between Wentworth and Louisa Musgrove) leads up to the final scenes where the happiness of the reunited lovers must still be contained within the social framework of an evening party. Although Anne attempts manoeuvres (at times as complex as a naval engagement!) in the revised scene of the proposal Wentworth achieves a sort of cutting-in operation. This style, in contrast with her own more retiring manner, had charmed Anne from the beginning; it is this comparison which leads her to reject the manners of her cousin William Elliott, which are 'polished, rational, discreet but not open'. (Elliott is a lawyer, a profession that Jane Austen does not favour. The vulgar Mrs Clay, whom he finally takes as his mistress, is the daughter of Sir Walter Elliott's solicitor or agent.)

> There never was any burst of feeling, or any warmth of indignation, or delight, at the evil or good of others. This, to Anne, was a decided imperfection. Her early impressions were incurable. She prized the frank, the open-hearted, the eager character beyond all others. Warmth and

enthusiasm did captivate her still. She felt she could so much more depend upon the sincerity of those who sometimes looked or said a careless or a hasty thing, than of those whose presence of mind never varied, whose tongue never slipped.

Events, of course, prove her more than justified. Her father's own manner exudes this careful chill; so does her sister's

'Very well,' said Elizabeth, 'I have nothing to send but my love . . . My best love, of course.'
'And mine,' added Sir Walter, 'kindest regards . . . make a civil message.'

At the other extreme, while Anne is trying to find out from Admiral Croft if Wentworth resents his friend's engagement to Louisa, the Admiral replies confidently '"Not at all, not at all; there is not an oath nor a murmur from beginning to end,"' and Anne has to persist a little: '"It might appear, you know, without its actually being said."'

Sincerity is a key word here, as in *Emma*. Lionel Trilling, studying it, declared that for a Frenchman sincerity means the recognition of such traits in himself as are morally or socially discrediting; to an Englishman it means that he communicates towards others without deception or misleading.[22] The naval contingent all practise sincerity, while the worldly men model themselves on Lord Chesterfield, and the necessity of dissimulation which he preached. Anne, sincere in the French sense, is constantly catching herself out in self-deception and gaining amusement from her own divided mind. In the end, Wentworth too sees that even his early resentment of Anne had been a disguised form of attachment. He had never forgotten her; she had so little forgotten him that it is his choice to stay aloof which has kept them apart for six of the eight years.

He had told his sister at first – while expecting contradiction – '"Anybody between fifteen and thirty may have me. A little beauty and a few smiles and a few compliments to the navy, and I am a lost man."' Anne had steadily preferred her dreary home to an escape through marriage:

No second attachment had been possible to the nice tone of her mind, the fastidiousness of her taste, in the small limits of society around her.

In the end he also can sincerely mock himself:

'Like other great men under reverses,' he answered with a smile, 'I must endeavour to suit my mind to my fortune. I must learn to brook being happier than I deserved.'

In this idyll the domestic life of the British Navy is thoroughly

vindicated against the squalors of Portsmouth in *Mansfield Park*, or
the wickedness of Admiral Crawford. Captain Harville's warm
defence, which draws out Anne's avowal of woman's constancy,
'when existence or when hope is gone', Captain Wentworth over-
hears with the quick ears of a lover and 'under the irresistible
governance of feelings' he responds forthwith by letter, so that they
come together at last as at first, in 'a room full of people and voices'.[23]
Here still, the reticence of the woman contrasts with the man's open
sincerity.

The one powerful relationship in this story, then, flows under or
through ordinary intercourse. Other relationships are subsidiary,
since the novel is almost exclusively given from Anne's point of view,
its frustrations and perplexities. Her promptitude of action and
warmth are balanced by Mary's weakness and Elizabeth's coldness;
but Anne moves out from the narrow confines of Kellynch and
Uppercross to Lyme and Bath (the recognised marriage-market for
such as her elder sister). The seasons move meanwhile from autumn
to spring, and Anne moves further towards the happiness depicted in
Wentworth's relatives, successors to her father at Kellynch Hall.
However, there is no close network of fine social ties such as Fanny or
Emma had experienced. Some minor characters are lightly sketched,
some situations just touched in.[24] The final revelation of her cousin
Elliott's duplicity comes through the squalid channels of Bath gossip.
Open irony diminishes any scenes that might overweigh minor
interests, and there are very sharp contrasts in varieties of grief. Mrs
Musgrove's sighings over her dead son depend on some forgetfulness
of what in life he had really inflicted on his family; his true nature is
forgotten, whereas Captain Harville's grief for his sister, silent but
undiminished, is shared by all; it marks the distinction 'between the
true and the not quite true'.[25]

A sharp burst of authorial mockery pricks the bubble 'catastrophe'
on the Cobbe at Lyme, and tells the alert reader that all will be well.

> By this time the report of the accident had spread among the workmen
> and boatmen about the Cobbe, and many were collected near them, to be
> useful if wanted, at any rate to enjoy the sight of a dead young lady, nay,
> two dead young ladies, for it proved twice as fine as the first report.

Anne mocks herself later when she imagines Lady Russell to be
gazing at Captain Wentworth, whereas it transpires only that she is
looking out for some special window curtains. As the heroine gains
in hope and confidence, the author detaches herself and prepares the
reader for Anne's passionate defence of constancy to Captain Harville
by giving her private reflections:

Prettier musings of high-wrought love and eternal constancy could never have passed along the streets of Bath than Anne was sporting with all the way from Camden Place to Westgate Buildings.

Gratified by Wentworth's open jealousy of William Elliott, Anne reflects with 'gratitude and respect, perhaps compassion' on the fact that Elliott must be rejected, for such was her feeling for Wentworth 'their union, she believed, could not divide her more from other men than their final separation'. Mr Elliott is fortunately on the point of being unmasked as 'black-hearted', the conventional villain; he is only part of the machinery. What he represents as a real temptation is the return to the past, the possession of Kellynch, the revival of her mother's name and title in herself. Here is that clinging to home that Fanny had felt so strongly. The temptation is offered by Lady Russell, and Anne rejects it. She mourned her mother still, but she is moving from out a dead world of social decorum, of which Lady Russell is also part.

Paradoxically this love-story, centred on the lovers, opens wider prospects. A sailor's wife may find herself anywhere in the world, as Mrs Crofts testifies: '"and I can safely say, the happiest part of my life has been spent on board ship. While we were together, you know, there was nothing to be feared."' Had she, eight years earlier, 'married to disoblige her family' like Mrs Price, Anne would have risked worldly disaster; but then she was not proposing to marry a Lieutenant Price! However, the contest between the world and the heart, in spite of all the pain involved, was also, for Anne, a contest of duty, her original act not merely one of compliance and retreat. Lady Russell stood 'in place of a parent' though her advice was not what Anne (or Mrs Musgrove or Mrs Crofts) would give. However, Captain Wentworth does not agree with her, and coolly says he may learn to forgive Lady Russell *in time*: not yet. Jane Austen is presenting a problem, not a rule of conduct here.

As the worldly counsel of prudence had earlier disrupted their union, so here the mere triviality of a social life led in public opposes its bulk like a physical obstacle. What a poet termed 'the universe of two' comes into being in spite of all the interposed rituals, and counterforces of decorum.

The greater variety of scene and the greater distinction between the world without and the world within are compatible with greater sensibility. ('One does not love a place less for having suffered in it', Anne remarks of Lyme to Wentworth.) They are part of Anne's developing freedom, her self-education, which leads her eventually to pass judgement on Lady Russell's views, and to choose detachment and the rôle of the teacher rather than the taught. In the end she joins a mobile society where she may yet have to face and share hardships beyond those of ordinary wives.

In the last sentence of this last novel, we learn that Anne's spring of felicity 'was in the warmth of her heart'. In tracing reticence rather than irony as the emerging characteristic of the later novels, I have attempted to suggest how much warmth lies behind their apparent coolness.

Notes

1 Tony Tanner, preface to *Mansfield Park* (Penguin English Classics); Kingsley Amis, 'What became of Jane Austen?'. (See *Jane Austen*, ed. Ian Watt, Prentice Hall, 1963.)

2 e.g. Marvin Mudrick, Wayne Booth in *The Rhetoric of Fiction* (Chicago, 1961); and Mark Schorer, in Ian Watt, op. cit.

3 Ed. Martha Vicinus, 1974; developed from a women's number of *Victorian Studies*.

4 Sir Thomas, at the ball, gives Henry Crawford a demonstration of Fanny's obedience by ordering her to bed.

5 E. M. Butler, '*Mansfield Park* and *Lovers' Vows*', *Modern Language Review* xxviii (1933), pp. 326–37.

6 See Claire Tomalin, *The Life and Death of Mary Wollstonecraft (1974)*, p. 215. Hannah More had castigated the work of Mrs Inchbald in her *Strictures on the Modern System of Female Education* (1799); although Mrs Inchbald's novel, *A Simple Story*, was known and approved by Jane Austen.

7 Lord Illingworth speaks in the very accents of the Crawfords: 'According to our ridiculous English laws I can't legitimize Gerald, but I can leave him my property. Illingworth is entailed of course, but it is a tedious barrack of a place. He can have Ashby, which is much prettier, Harborough which has the best shooting in the North of England, and the house in St James's square . . . you can have whatever allowance you like and live where you choose', he tells his former mistress.

8 As her son, Henry Crawford was allowed more physical outlet than in many a lover's part; as Mary Crawford tartly observes, these two indefatigable rehearsers are always trying *not* to embrace. The acting is physically as dangerous to Maria's feelings as to Mary's.

9 Lionel Trilling, *Sincerity and Authenticity* (1972) p. 79.

10 C. S. Lewis, 'A Note on Jane Austen', in Ian Watts (see Note I): *Essays in Criticism*, no. IV (October 1954). I replied to this in no. VI with 'A Note on Fanny Price', from which some of the following points are taken.

11 I owe this point to Mary Lascelles, preface to *Mansfield Park*. It is handled polemically by Patricia Beer in *Reader I Married Him* (Macmillan, 1974) p. 74.

12 I owe this and several other points to Mary Lascelles, *Jane Austen and her Art* (Oxford University Press, 1939).

13 However Lady Bertram can prick Mrs Norris's protests of poverty with

devastating simplicity; she is perhaps a shade brighter than Mrs Price.

14 Patricia Beer finds it perfectly sensible, even wise. (op. cit., p. 84) At that moment? to that person?

15 Emma also prepared to hear Mr Knightley tell her he loved Harriet.

16 At the Modern Language Association's meeting in Adelaide, August 1974.

17 Anthony Trollope termed it cowardice (*Casebook*, p. 52).

18 Emma had told Frank Churchill her suspicions of Jane and Mr Dixon; Harriet had been a 'sacrifice to conjugal unreserve' between the Eltons.

19 As Fanny had been Edmund's confidant, and Anne was everybody's.

20 In Jane Austen love at first sight is never met. All her lovers are already thoroughly familiar with each other, except in *Northanger Abbey*, her first novel.

21 Lesbianism was considered a 'dirty little vice of servant girls, boarding school and actresses' (Claire Tomalin, *The Life and Death of Mary Wollstonecraft*, p. 18, citing Mrs Piozzi's diary.) In 1746 Henry Fielding published an account of a recent case, *The Female Husband*.

22 Lionel Trilling, *Sincerity and Authenticity* (Oxford University Press, 1972).

23 As in *Emma*, Jane Fairfax and Frank Churchill had been estranged in a room full of people.

24 A point of irony is to give the widow, Mrs Clay, the name which above all symbolises what Anne stands for – Penelope, constant to the absent sailor.

25 See Mary Lascelles, *Jane Austen and her Art* (Oxford University Press, 1939) p. 80. Captain Wentworth emphasises this by saying no one would have mourned for *him*, had he been lost in his leaky first command, the *Asp*.

III.

Barbara Bodichon, George Eliot and the Limits of Feminism

Those who would wish to propound a 'wave theory' for the general advance of women's emancipation in England might note, as Barbara Bodichon had noted by 1857, that in the second half of the eighteenth century and again the second half of the nineteenth century, advance began with an educational improvement; in social rather than in legislative changes. The pattern has emerged again through what some universities term 'women studies' – which in one American university has led to the supplementing of that biased subject *his*tory by a course designated *her*story.

In the eighteenth century, the year 1745 saw the birth of Hannah More, model of energy and propriety, who made her fortune (and those of her four sisters) out of a Bristol school, founded a whole chain of village schools, wrote sermons, novels as well as penny tracts to guard the peasantry against the pernicious doctrines of Tom Paine, and

> the holy dramas of Miss Hannah More
> Where all the nine and little Moses snore.

Dr Johnson termed her 'the most powerful versificatrix in the English language' (a characteristic backhander), and Cobbett 'the old Bishop in petticoats'.

On the extreme left wing, among *The Unsexed Females* (1798) denounced by the Rev. Richard Polwhele, he could

> See Wollstonecraft, whom no decorum checks,
> Arise, the intrepid champion of sex.

But before 'each heartbeat in the Paphian grove' (i.e., in revolutionary Paris) 'beat quick to Imlay and licentious love' she too had kept a school, as her sisters continued to do. That impassioned, incoherent and rambling manifesto, *A Vindication of the Rights of Women*

(1792) placed the citoyenne as natural leader of the little feminist group in London who were attempting to live by their pen – Mrs Inchbald, Mrs Fenwick, Mary Hays, philosophess. In her life of Mary Wollstonecraft (1759–97) Claire Tomalin has recently illuminated the absurdities and heroics of a pioneer; her courage, her capacity for self-dramatisation, her determination to 'impose her will on fate'.

Among the aristocracy, the era of the blue-stockings was succeeded by that of such extraordinary Romantics as the Ladies of Llangollen, who eloped together from Ireland in 1778 to a Welsh valley where they set up a rural retreat of the utmost privacy on the main road to Holyhead; for fifty years dressed as men, cultivated sensibility, and forgot to pay their bills. They were contemporary with Hannah More, but compared with her Lilies of the Field, who demonstrated their emancipation by their mode of living, to be far outclassed by Lady Hester Stanhope, niece and hostess of the younger Pitt who, blighted by the death of Sir John Moore at Corunna, removed herself in 1810 to the Lebanon where she exercised a despotism that quelled her visitors, and a power of conversation that sometimes caused them to faint of fatigue. These ladies lived out their revolutionary existences without theorising, and example can be more potent than exhortation; the independence of 'The English Miss' became an example to Europe, as the American girl was to become a challenge to English women.

Educator, would-be legislator, pioneer of a new life style, Barbara Bodichon fulfilled all these roles, and I am concerned to suggest here in her the beginnings of a more complex feminism than the traditional kind.

It was not until the late 1840s that modest signs of a feminist revival reappeared: 1848, the year of revolution in Europe, saw in England the revolutionary founding of a decorous college for women (Queen's College, Harley Street) by a young socialist cleric; although in the previous year, in *The Princess*, Alfred Tennyson had let woman out of the cage – only to shut her in again. The new women of the 1850s emerged again as a group; most powerfully as an educational group in London. Alicia Percival termed them '*A Remarkable Set*'. The first moves towards legal – as distinct from social – reform were led by Barbara Leigh Smith, a young woman who, as the daughter of a prominent family of parliamentarians, was in a strong position to exercise the many talents, and use the ample fortune with which she was endowed.

Her grandfather had been a lieutenant of William Wilberforce. A wealthy London merchant and a Unitarian, her father fought for the repeal of the Corn Laws; he gave to Barbara a liberal education. Born in 1827 she was his eldest child and grew up commandingly beautiful with blue eyes and red-gold hair. She early developed a talent for painting which, although a fashionable accomplishment for any young lady, with her became a profession by which she earned a small fortune. Accompanied only by a young friend, the equally emancipated grand-daughter of Joseph Priestley, Miss Bessie Parkes, she went on a sketching tour of Europe.

In 1854 this young woman of twenty-five, spirited, gay, adventurous, caused a sensation with a trenchant tract on the laws of property as they related to married women. *A Brief Summary in Plain Language*, compiled with the aid of the Recorder of Birmingham, is totally devoid of the incoherent, choked anger which had marked earlier the manifesto of Mary Wollstonecraft. It sold for a few pence. Exposing the position under common law (to some extent redressed under equity) it explained that in the almost total submergence of a married woman's legal identity, her body belonged to her husband, and he could enforce his right by a writ of *habeas corpus*; that without consent a married woman or even a betrothed woman might not dispose of any property; that on marriage all her personal property passed to her husband, including her earnings, whether they were living together or not (though for women of the upper class, marriage settlements afforded an expensive chance of protection). Sections on divorce and women as trustees followed. A married woman might by permission make a will, but her husband might revoke it at any time before probate. She had no legal rights over her children. This section ends with the contemptuous privileges that accrue; a woman could not be accused of burglary, housebreaking or arson if committed under her husband's influence, or be found guilty of theft from her husband or of setting his house on fire as in law they were one person.

The last section concerns unmarried mothers and their children.

> The rights of an illegitimate child are only such as he can acquire; he can inherit nothing, being in law looked on as nobody's son, but he may acquire property by devising or bequest. He may acquire a surname by reputation but does not inherit one . . .
>
> The only incapacity under which he labours is that he cannot be heir at law or next of kin to any person, nor can he have any heirs except lineal descendants; if he acquire property and die without a will, such property will go to the crown unless he leaves a lineal descendant.

Here may be discerned the personal impulse behind Barbara's campaign, for she and her brother and sisters were illegitimate. Her father, Benjamin Leigh Smith, at the age of forty, had encountered a pretty milliner's apprentice, Anne Longden, and in Barbara's phrase, 'notorious cohabitation as man and wife' followed.

On her coming of age, her father had settled £300 a year on her – a freedom which the greatest heiress did not often enjoy. Yet although her official biography, written in 1949, concealed it, she had no right to the family coat of arms or the name by which she was known. As she dearly loved her father the inner conflict must have been severe. Mrs Gaskell noted that 'she is – in consequence, I think of her birth – a strong fighter against the established opinions of the world. I can't help admiring her noble bravery and respecting while I personally don't like her.'[1]

Barbara indeed in some ways resembled the noble eccentrics of a previous generation; she dressed unconventionally, she silenced the opposition with a masculine 'Bosh!', and drove off visitors with 'Devastators of the day, away, away!'

The year 1854 was notable in larger ways than by Barbara's tract. It was the year of the war in the Crimea, invaded in September by the French and British. On 4 November, the eve of the Battle of Inkerman and ten days after Balaclava, Barbara's first cousin, Florence Nightingale, landed at Scutari Base Hospital; backed with the resources of *The Times*, she not only directed the nursing but set about feeding and clothing the British Army. Another cousin, Lady Verney, could write in 1856,

> What Florence has done towards raising the standards of women's capabilities and work is most important. It is quite curious how everyday questions regarding them are answered quite differently from what they would have been eighteen months ago![2]

However, the Nightingales did not acknowledge or call on their illegitimate cousins, who remained 'the *tabooed* family'.[3] There is no evidence of how her cousin's achievement struck Barbara Leigh Smith, except that after her marriage she proudly recorded her husband's wish to meet only those members of her family who had known them as children.

Barbara first proved her paternity by taking the direct route to legislative change. Her pamphlet on married women's property ends with an appeal to support the Law Amendment Society, but three years later, in 1857, their proposals were defeated in the House. (1870 saw the first, inadequate, legislation.)

Signatures collected by Barbara in support of the Bill for a Married Women's Property Act included 3000 literary ladies; the Law Amendment Society had collected in all 24,000 signatures and uncovered new and horrifying cases of victimisation, but the reviews showed the forces of prejudice.

> 'So long as the petticoat rebellion was confined to a mistaken petition of a few literary ladies whose peculiar talents placed them in a rather anoma-

lous position', remarked the *Saturday Review*, 'we really had not the heart to say anything serious about it.'

But the Law Amendment Society's proposals 'set at defiance the experience of every country in Christendom and the common sense of mankind'. So the petition from among others Mrs Browning, Mrs Carlyle, Mrs Gaskell and George Eliot went for nothing. The women had gained experience; they had enlisted the support of some generous members of Parliament; they had spoken up.

Barbara was even then preparing a desperate and rather incoherent pamphlet entitled *Women and Work*. In great contrast with her first tract, it bears all the marks of protest, in shapeless accumulation of harrowing examples introduced by a manifesto which proclaimed 'Women may not take a man as god; they must not hold their first duty to be towards any human being.'

> Look at unmarried women of thirty-five – the prime of life. Do you know one who is healthy and happy? If you do, she is one who has found her work. (*Women and Work* (1857) p. 13)

Then we hear of two girls bereaved of their lovers – one lost her reason instantly and never recovered it, the other cried, 'My God, if I had anything to do, I could bear this grief.' Various employments are recommended: the Post Office, the electric telegraph, teaching, accountancy and nursing. A series of letters illustrates women's search for a medical education – still in progress.

The pamphlet, designed as one of a series by 'English women and American men', first came out in the *Englishwomen's Journal* (founded by Barbara and Bessie Parkes) in February 1857. Barbara was now surrounded by many helpers who ran her journal, an employment agency which started in its offices, and her free-discipline school for poor children. An enthusiastic friend painted her as Boadicea; she had become the feminist leader. But by the end of the 1850s all had changed; married to a Frenchman, after visiting negro chapels in the slave States of North America, sailing down the Mississippi, drawing, sketching, fending off the attentions of a mad Texan general, she had settled for half the year in the exotic exile of Algiers. She was by no means simply a Lily of the Field however. By the end of the next decade she had played a leading part in the first campaign for the enfranchisement of women, and through another fortunate friendship, become one of the founders of what was to be Girton College.

Since she did not show the single-mindedness of other feminists she has been dubbed 'Amateur, advanced'.[4] The lack of a single commitment seems to me, on the contrary, to be her rare and peculiar strength. She could be vigorous, masculine – Rossetti's 'good fellow';

she could be deeply sympathetic, with the intuitive sympathies of the artist. The vitality which sustained her was fed directly into the work of her closest friend, George Eliot; thus her powers expressed themselves in what a modern poet has termed 'nutrition of impulse'.

Barbara rejected that 'Taboo on tenderness' which their causes imposed on Florence Nightingale and Emily Davies. They were ruthless towards their helpers, intransigent (as they had to be); Barbara's pamphlet on *Women at Work*, written at the height of her own personal crisis, shows personal stress but is the less effectual for that reason. In her determination not to forgo or suppress any side of her nature, she endured the conflict of interests that is more common today. So in a sense the rhythm of her life is the rhythm of the third wave of feminism. It is then to Barbara's personal life that I now turn. For much of the new knowledge I am indebted to the labours of Gordon Haight on the life and letters of George Eliot.

Barbara and Marian

The literary sensation of 1859, a novel by a new novelist, was *Adam Bede*; 14,000 copies could not nearly meet the demand. It was being translated into many languages and there was 'a ring of applause in all directions' as her publisher told the author. But the identity of that author was kept a close secret. While all London was speculating – one or two had hazarded that it was a woman – a letter from Algiers reached Marian Lewes:

26 April 1859

My darling Marian,
Forgive me for being so very affectionate but I am so intensely delighted with your success. I have got *The Times* of April 12th with the glorious review of 'Adam Bede' and a few days ago I read the *Westminster Review* article. I can't tell you how I triumphed in the triumph you have made. It is so great a one. Now you see I have not as yet got the book, but I know that it is you. I read one long extract which instantly made me internally exclaim 'that is written by Marian Evans . . .' Now the more I get of the book, the more certain I am, not because it is like what you have written before, but because it is like what I see in you. 'It is an opinion which fire cannot melt out of me, I would die in it at the stake' . . .

That YOU, *that you* whom they spit at should do it!

I am so enchanted with the good and bad of me! Both angel and devil triumph! (*Haight*, iii. 56)[5]

This intuitive brilliance of conviction and generous warmth of response was quite unparalleled. No one else perceived what she at once saw. Marian Lewes replied to her friend's letter:

> God bless you, dearest Barbara, for your love and sympathy. You are the first friend who has given any symptom of knowing me – the first heart that has recognised me in a book that has come from my heart of hearts. But keep the secret solemnly till I give you leave to tell it, and give way to no impulse of triumphant affection . . . Your letter today gave me more joy, more heart glow than all the letters or reviews or other testimonies of success that have come to me since the evening I read aloud my manuscripts to my dear husband and he laughed and cried alternately and then rushed to kiss me. He is the prime blessing that has made all the rest possible to me – giving me a response to everything I have written, a response that I could confide in as a proof that I had not mistaken my work. (*Haight*, iii. 63–5)

And George Lewes added a postscript, 'Dear Barbara – you are a darling!', while warning her not to write about Marian Evans who had been for ever replaced by Marian Lewes.

This deep, instinctive rapport between two artists did not need strengthening by florid expression or even regular intercourse. Based on striking similarities in two lives outwardly rather different, it was to remain to the end. Marian could speak to this friend as to no other. It was to Barbara that she made her confession of faith at its most dramatic: 'The highest calling and election is *to do without opium*, and live through all our pain with conscious, clear-eyed endurance' (*Haight*, iii. 366), while to others she spoke more mildly of 'doing without consolation'.

The two had first met eight years before in 1852, and Barbara was immediately struck by the shy, gauche young prodigy from the Midlands, who in turn was gratified by the impression she had made on 'your noble looking friend, Barbara', as she told Bessie Parkes. When in July 1854 George Lewes and Marian Evans went abroad together to live as man and wife, Bessie's radical father, 'white with rage', forbade correspondence, but when after a year they returned, Barbara wrote a letter so expressive of 'her strong, noble nature' that Marian, in sending it to a friend, desired it should be destroyed. This, however, may have been as much on Barbara's account as her own, for both these women had been the victims of attentions from the notorious John Chapman, and in the summer of 1855 Barbara was struggling with his proposal that she should go to live with him in an extra-marital union.

In 1851 the handsome and winning editor of the *Westminster Review* had invited Marian Evans to share his home with his long-suffering wife and his mistress. When the mistress found Chapman and Marian Evans holding hands she created such a scene that, supported by the wife, she obliged Marian Evans, after a month of intense discomfort – for her feelings had been involved quite deeply – to retire to Coventry. It was in the trough of this experience that Barbara and Marian met. Three years later the Chapmans, as neighbours of the Leigh Smiths, took Barbara's Aunt Julia as their boarder. In the midst of her campaign for securing married women's property, in the autumn Barbara's health suddenly broke down under the stress.[6] With her aunt and sisters she wintered in Rome and returned to painting. By August 1855 Chapman was suggesting that in the interests of her health they should become lovers; he claimed some medical authority, urged Barbara to tell her women friends. They corresponded, and met in Sussex, but there is no evidence and little likelihood that Barbara was engaged in a liaison, as one writer has suggested.[7] Chapman's letters for August and September 1855 survive only in transcript, but he pleads 'the reinvigorating effect on your system of a fulfilment of love's physical desires' which would be 'the healthiest and surest means of recovery'. This is the language of wooing, not of conquest.

The level of Chapman's hypocrisy can be measured by his appeal to Barbara to 'try to be hopeful and peaceful. Rely upon it, we shall be happy yet. Lewes and M.E. seem perfectly so.' Yet ten months earlier he had written of these two to Robert Chambers:

> I should be sorry to be thought to disparage her . . . I think him much the most blameworthy in the matter. Now I can only pray, against hope, that he may prove constant to her; otherwise she is *utterly* lost. She has a noble nature, which in good circumstances and under good influences would have shone out. (Haight, *George Eliot, a Biography*, 1968, p. 167)

His letters indicate that Chapman was by no means indifferent to Barbara's fortune. Having undergone bankruptcy, he was in chronic financial difficulties. His enquiries about her money are almost as specific as his enquiries about the physical details of her malady (the general taboo on such subjects has recently been shown in a collection of essays edited by Martha Vicinus, *Suffer and Be Still*). If Barbara would explain to her family what they proposed 'You would then maintain your right and equal relations with them, and would be able without fear and undue anxiety and without the knowledge of the world to be really united with me, and look forward with joyous anticipation to become a Mother.' (How this last was to be effected without the knowledge of the world was not explained.)

Chapman was presumably expecting that a man who had reared five illegitimate children would not object to illegitimate unions, but when Barbara broached the subject of free-love to her father in general terms, he told her if she wanted to practise it she ought to go to the New World. And when she finally explained Chapman's proposition he was furious, though it seems to have been Barbara's brother who persuaded her to give up 'her accursed love'.

It was likely that when next year (1856) Barbara visited Tenby, her friend Marian could speak of sorrow and renunciation with understanding, and perhaps also bestow some consolation. It would appear that the two women exchanged intimate confidences. Marian noted in her journal:

> We enjoyed her society very much but were deeply touched to see that three years had made her so much older and sadder. Her activity for great objects is admirable and contact with her is a fresh inspiration to work while it is day. (ibid., p. 205)

For a second winter (1856–7) the sisters, under the escort of their brother, went abroad, this time to Algiers.

On 14 April 1857 Barbara announced her engagement to Eugène Bodichon, a French physician eighteen years her senior, who had lived for many years in Algiers and had campaigned for the abolition of slavery there. The Leweses were not quite happy (*Haight*, ii. 320), the Smith family decidedly cool, but on 2 July 1857, at the Little Portland Street Chapel, Barbara Leigh Smith, 'artist', was married. Before setting off for a year-long tour of the United States, the Bodichons dined with the Leweses and Marian wrote to a friend 'we think the *essential* is there'. Her father made a most generous settlement on Barbara, who was given the full protection of the law; from her journal it appears that he had visited the United States when Barbara was an infant; perhaps had even thought of settling there with his common-law wife.

With some naïvety, it appears that Barbara had expected that Dr Bodichon might be persuaded to settle and practise in England. But as he never learned English, and had no intention of being uprooted, Barbara perforce became a part-time colonist – and in a French not an English colony. She commuted, spending about half the year abroad.

Her marriage bestowed an unequivocal social position. In France her doubtful birth would not be known to any. Everyone called her 'ma cousine' at the family home in Brittany. Dr Bodichon's father was a professional man, his mother came of an aristocratic family; she cherished his family tree and coat of arms, keeping them with her marriage lines and her painter's medals as the most precious of personal possessions.[8] There was enough wealth to dispel all thought of fortune hunting; 'Boadicea' once told a friend that she had married her doctor because he reminded her of Caractacus, and was really an ancient Briton. The eccentric Dr Bodichon ministered to colonists and natives alike, wore Arab dress, wrote huge unreadable tomes about humanity at large, believed in euthanasia. Yet, by his complete readiness to let his wife manage her affairs in her own way, he gave her security with the minimum of restriction. Long before she had proclaimed her desire to mix with 'the oddities of this world', and eventually she chose to marry one. Later, Barbara said she wished for three lives – one to live with the Doctor, one as an artist, one to use for social reforms. The rhythm of her life was part of 'the wave of the future'.

In union Marian Evans had found a constant solicitude that protected her from adverse criticism. Lewes suppressed all unfavourable reviews, and 'produced' her like an impresario. Barbara found freedom in the exotic beauty of Algiers (but only for half the year), an honourable escape for the artist from the demands of social conscience – the equivalent of Marian's chosen seclusion.

Not very long after the great success of *Adam Bede*, the Leweses became neighbours of Barbara who had inherited her father's house in Blandford Square. As soon as she returned to Algiers Barbara began to explore the possibility of George Lewes obtaining a divorce under French law. This turned out impossible, but Marian wrote:

> I am not sorry. I think the boys will not suffer, and for myself I prefer excommunication. I have no earthly thing that I care for, to gain by being brought within the pale of people's personal attention, and I have many things to care for that I should lose – my freedom from petty worldly torments, commonly called pleasures, and that isolation which really keeps my charity warm, instead of chilling it, as much contact with frivolous women would do.[9]

This concealed form of exile or emigration became an essential protective device. It was in this same year also that first Marian and then Barbara were to sit for the portrait painter Samuel Lawrence. These portraits shew a lively determined Barbara, a pensive and melancholy Marian.[10] Yet by the end of the 1850s, Marian, at forty, secure in a worldly sense, had discovered her full power as an artist. She set to work on a highly ambitious novel, in which the central figure combined many ideals, but more especially was it a portrait of her fellow artist.

In 1862, Marian had written to Barbara:

> These are the results that give one fortitude to endure one's enemies – even to endure one's friends. I will not call you a friend – I will rather call you by some name that I am not obliged to associate with evaporated professions and petty egotism. I will call you only Barbara, the name I must always associate with a true large heart. Some mean treacherous

Barbara may come across me, but she will be only like a shadow of a vulgar woman flitting across my fresco of St Barbara. (*Haight*, ii. 119)

It was at this period that she set to work on *Romola*. On 1 January 1862, George Eliot noted in her diary the beginning; on Tuesday, 9 June 1863, she recorded 'Put the last stroke to *Romola*. Ebenezer!' (*Haight*, iv. 87).

The heroine of this ambitious study bears an unmistakeable physical likeness to 'the gorgeous Barbara'. Many characters are visually conceived; at the opening of chapter IV we first meet the tall figure with beautiful red-gold hair, the snood or fillet, the square-cut neckline of Barbara's portrait:

> a tall maiden of seventeen or eighteen, who was standing before a carved *leggio* or reading desk, such as is often seen in the choirs of Italian churches. The hair was of a reddish gold colour, enriched by an unbroken small ripple such as may be seen in the sunset clouds on grandest autumnal evenings. It was confined by a black fillet above her small ears, from which it rippled forward again, and made a natural veil for her neck above her square cut gown of rascia or black serge . . .
>
> There was the same refinement of brow and nostril . . . counterbalanced by a full though firm mouth and a powerful chin, which gave an expression of proud tenacity and latent impetuousness; an expression carried out in the backward poise of the girl's head and the grand line of her neck and shoulders. It was a type of face of which one could not venture to say whether it would inspire love or only that unwilling admiration which is mingled with dread.

The last phrase shows that more than physical characteristics were modelled from Barbara, for it suggests the kind of impression made on Mrs Gaskell: 'I can't help admiring her noble bravery and respecting her, while I don't personally like her.'

In the last chapter the passage of time is recorded.

> An eager life had left its marks upon her; the finely moulded cheeks had sunk a little, the golden crown was less massive; but there was a placidity in Romola's face that had never belonged to it in youth. It is but once that we can know our worst sorrows and Romola had known them while life was new.

George Eliot expatiated at length on the relation of the real and the imaginative in this novel, saying 'Any real observation of life and character must be limited and the imagination must fill in and give life to the picture' (*Haight*, iii. 427). She also knew that she had idealised Romola. Her friend Sara Hennell felt that anyone so loved and so wanted must be worshipped as a 'beautiful saint' (*Haight*, iv. 104).

George Eliot, 'struck by the painful truth' of this sketch, replied:

You are right in saying Romola is ideal – I feel it acutely in the reproof my own soul is constantly getting from the image it has made. My own books scourge me.

F. R. Leavis has observed: Romola in fact, is another, idealized George Eliot – less real than Maggie Tulliver and more idealized. While patrician and commandingly beautiful, she has also George Eliot's combination of intellectual power, emancipation, inherent piety and hunger for exaltation. (*The Great Tradition*, p. 48)

These features, however, are partly Barbara's; for in this idealised figure the two images are superimposed. *Romola* is an idealising of the women's cause, not only in the character of its heroine but in the claims for feminist culture implicit in the writing of the book itself.[11]

The deep centre of the book comes not in Romola nor in Savonarola, but in Tito. Although the start was agonisingly slow, George Eliot eventually records 'killed Tito in great excitement'. As a study in degeneration, the handsome, winning, artistic youth, with all his charm, and his fatal desire to make life easy, recalls Arthur Donnithorne and Squire Cass, but it could be surmised that as Tito stands between the lovely patrician and the simple *contadina*, both of whom he has deceived, so Marian Lewes was enjoying her revenge on the man who had shewn such complete selfishness in his relations with both Barbara and herself. The figure of Dr John Chapman has been detected behind Romola's sense of betrayal by previous critics; but his presence becomes more definite if it is recognised that both figures projected in the heroine had in real life suffered much the same betrayal from this same individual.[12]

The fall of Tito, the 'live' part of this story, tells of a man who betrayed his benefactor for money and power. The marketing of this book involved its author in the slickest money transaction of her upright life. A 'mean, treacherous Marian' momentarily flits like a shadow across the noble saintly image of George Eliot. The novels that spelt affluence for her had all been published hitherto by *Blackwood's Magazine*; but *Romola* was at the last moment transferred, for a huge bribe, to the firm of Smith Elder and Co. and the rival *Cornhill*. In an interview with the gentlemanly John Blackwood, Marian betrayed an agonising sense of shame (*Haight*, iv. 38, 44); he blamed the 'voracity' of Lewes. Marian Evans herself had been bred in the careful scrupulous habit of one of her own Midland farming characters; she would apologise for sending a letter without a stamp, would write that Barbara had dropped a handkerchief which would be kept against her return, and would also remind her that she had borrowed a shilling from the Leweses' maid to pay for a cab fare and ask her to refund it. Barbara was generous and open in the way that comes more easily to one who has never had to count her pennies.

Romola was an ambitious novel, and the 'masculine protest' of its claims is patent. George Eliot had read Walter Scott, and to that traditional model of dignity she added the weight of learning, reading Italian history, visiting Florence, studying dialects, filling a triple series of notebooks, aided by Lewes, who however had to reassure her that 'she knows infinitely more of Savonarola than she did of Silas' (*Haight*, iii. 420) while insisting that a romance is not the product of an encyclopedia (*Haight*, iii. 473–4). Unsuccessful as art, *Romola* marked some kind of inner gestation that enabled the writer to move on to greater things, as Ibsen spent ten years on the ambitious *Emperor and Galilean* before he achieved *A Doll's House*. This work was necessary to the author, and belongs to her biography.

* * *

In spite of Barbara's absence in Algiers, she contrived to exert her practical kindness on behalf of George Lewes's sons, looking after the elder when he began to work in London (*Haight*, iii. 342), helping to send the second, 'a difficult young bear', to farm in Natal, and when he returned, mortally ill, to be nursed by Marian, visiting, sending delicacies, condoling with the Leweses when at last he died (*Haight*, v. 60–1). Her own childlessness was a heavy grief to Barbara.

By the mid-1860s she once more attacked the citadel of legislation, this time in the cause of votes for women. The educational movement had already gathered great momentum. In 1865 John Stuart Mill had been elected to Parliament, Barbara driving round Westminster in his support, accompanied by Bessie Parkes, (now Madame Belloc) and a new friend, met in Algiers, a Miss Emily Davies, who had wintered there to nurse a sick brother. Shortly after, Barbara read a paper on Women's Suffrage to an influential women's club. Another petition, asking for votes for women, was organised. When, at the last moment, Mme Bodichon fell ill, Emily Davies, accompanied by Dr Elizabeth Garrett, on 7 June 1866 carried the scroll with 1500 signatures to Mill at the House. A movement had been born; associations were formed; and on 20 May 1867 Mill rose to move an amendment to the Representation of the People Bill. His amendment (of course) was lost, by 194 to 73 votes. Once again Mme Bodichon had helped to start a movement which was not to come to fruition for many years, although in 1869 Mill contributed further to the cause by publishing *The Subjection of Women*. However, reverting from the legislative to the social and to experiment in the now traditional sphere of education, Barbara was to establish what was to prove her single public feminist victory and monument. Miss Emily Davies, after first enquiring anxiously if it would be proper to do so, went to call on Mrs Lewes at Blandford Square. The spiritual descendant of Hannah More, Miss Davies was highly conservative in every direction but one. She had become secretary of a group for founding a women's college which should aim exclusively at giving the highest education to girls. Mme Bodichon had made a generous donation, besides giving plentifully of her advice and enthusiasm. The doors opened at Hitchin in 1869. 'You must make your own laws', Barbara told the students.

Emily Davies and Barbara Bodichon had set up the first college for the university education of women. In four years it was moved from its original site to Cambridge, and was then renamed Girton College.

Marian wrote to 'dearest B.' in Algiers that although she was much occupied 'the better education of women is one of the objects about which I have *no doubt*' (*Haight*, iv. 399), and 'the Author of *Romola*' subscribed £50, while a note was sent from Mr and Mrs Lewes

> that we strongly object to the proposal that there should be a beginning made 'on a small scale' . . . everyone concerned should be roused to understand that a great campaign is being victualled for. (*Haight*, iv. 401)

From the beginning the college attracted women internationally, and sent out its graduates to regions far remoter than Algiers. Later, Marian was moved to offer a scholarship to aid Barbara's work, and in one of the students she found another model.

Sarah Marks, a daughter of a poor Polish immigrant, had worked as a governess till she was rescued by Mme Bodichon. Destined to a brilliant career as a physicist, to become the friend of Mme Curie and the first woman proposed for membership of the Royal Society, she was also the model for the Jewish heroine Mirah, of *Daniel Deronda*.[13] However when, in the summer of 1877, another Girton student, Miss Henrietta Müller, invited Marian to visit Girton, a storm blew up. In May she wrote to Barbara, with restrained anger:

> I have been rather annoyed by Mr Lewes having told me yesterday that some unpleasantness had arisen between Miss Barnard [the Mistress] and the students at Girton about the invitation sent to me . . . Mr Lewes says you suggested my calling to see the College in the ordinary way, but this affair with Miss Barnard makes me disinclined to appear there at all. (*Haight*, vi. 734)

Lewes had been protecting her, as he always did, but it is said she drove in by the back drive only. Lord Lawrence's niece would not meet 'Mrs Lewes'.

In the very month of this betrayal from within, Barbara, who was staying in north Cornwall to paint, was smitten by severe paralysis and temporarily lost the use of speech. Sarah Marks asked to be allowed to nurse her and eventually went, sending news to Marian, who seemed unable to associate any fear with so vital a creature though she had often poured out dreams about death (*Haight*, iv. 362, 237). She wrote now casually, asking if Barbara could help in finding a governess for some Cambridge friends, or whether Miss Scott (Girton's most distinguished mathematician) could find her a housekeeper? However, the deeper note crept back when Marian wrote in October 1878

> I miss so much the hope I used to have of seeing you in London and talking over everything, just as we used to do – in the way that will never come exactly with anyone else. (*Haight*, vii, 70–1)

When, a month afterwards, George Lewes died, Barbara wrote tenderly, and received a tender reply – the first letter Marian could pen under the shock.

The final exchange of the two is perhaps the most revealing; Barbara was one of the five people to whom Marian wrote, rather stiffly, on the eve of her marriage to Johnny Cross, whom she had been used to address as 'nephew', and who was twenty years her junior. In a Freudian piece of forgetfulness, the letter was never posted, but Barbara sent an exquisite and tactful note.

> My dear, I hope and I think you may be happy . . . you see I know all love is so different, that I do not see it as unnatural to love in new ways. If I knew Mr Lewes, he would be as glad as I am.

The reply was warm, as Marian dwelt on 'the wonderful blessing falling on me beyond my share, after I had thought that my life was ended.' Six months later she too had died, and the London clubmen were mocking the disconsolate Johnny Cross as 'George Eliot's widow', but Barbara Bodichon faced the long diminishing of another decade of pain.[14]

What, as an artist, did she accomplish in that third of her life? Though she studied with Holman Hunt and later worked in Paris at Corot's studio, Barbara remained an artist on a small scale. Her work gives the same kind of pleasure as minor Elizabethan pastoral; delicate water colours, studies primarily of light, show a muted palette of subtle greys, greens, browns and blues. Life in Africa could but deepen her appreciation of the tones and colours on mountain, desert and littoral. The tranquillity of her landscapes is quite at variance with her energetic and striking public activities. Within her art she developed the more feminine and contemplative aspects of her talent; here, she escaped from the conscience that in her daily life pressed upon her. She remained the recorder of a mood of sun and shadow, an organic natural whole of sky, sea and earth sustained by Corot's maxim 'Il faut chercher les valeurs.'

She held exhibitions, and earned £10,000, bequeathed to Girton College; but Ruskin wrote to her playfully and waspishly about her American tour; he thought Louisiana swamps unworthy of artistic study. From his point of view, an Algerian scene would perhaps be little better. What finally was left to posterity by the woman with 'face both sad and bright' whom a young cousin called 'a genius little known and soon forgot'? It is hard to tell, because she instigated so many movements and worked through so many lives. She was no slave of a career; but I would think that what was 'thoroughly finished', what yields the 'true glory', was her experiment in balanced living. This began in youth, with her little free-discipline school, with the building of a weekend cottage at Scalands; out of these grew the life of Cambridge and Algiers.

Barbara's example changed the climate of opinion, not instantly, as did Florence Nightingale's, but stealthily, like the influence of the weather. She was always concerned that the work should be done rather than that she should achieve anything by it for herself; she was even prepared, which is rarer, to initiate movements which she thought could not hope to be completed in her time. The stress and disappointment that counterbalanced her energy are most movingly revealed in a long letter of sympathy she wrote to her cousin Hilary Bonham Carter:

> You must take the second best, on which I live myself, always feeling that there is some way of solving the riddle of the suffering world that I cannot see . . . If I bear the troubles and get on in life at all . . . it is on . . . a sort of rough wooden scaffold bridge of life, where some day I hope to see a perfect arch.[15]

Notes

1 Letter to Charles Eliot Norton (*Letters*, ed. Jane Whitehall, 1932, p. 52). I have heard that Barbara learnt of her illegitimacy only at seventeen.
2 G. Trevelyan, *British History in the Nineteenth Century*, p. 307n.
3 G. Haight, *Letters of George Eliot* (ii. 45). This is evidence of how far the social disability of illegitimacy was acknowledged, for Marian Evans is speaking on very slight acquaintance.
4 By Alicia Percival.
5 *The Letters of George Eliot*, ed. Gordon Haight, 7 vols (Oxford 1954–5) referred to throughout as *Haight*.
6 I have been informed that there was a family history of mental instability.

7 Joseph W. Reed, Jr (ed.), *The American Diary, 1857–8*, Routledge, 1972, p. 32. An unsympathetic work, further handicapped by lack of acquaintance with the nuances of English society.

8 The collection was recently acquired by Girton College, Cambridge.

9 Bessie Parkes also sought this kind of freedom by marrying, to Barbara's distress, the invalid Frenchman Louis Belloc; she became the mother of Hilaire Belloc and Mrs Belloc Lowndes. Her papers are now at Girton College.

10 Both at Girton College, Cambridge.

11 Many scene are depicted in pictorial terms. Romola, appearing to the villagers with the gypsy baby reclining on her arm, is presented as an icon – almost a Sistine Madonna.

12 Marian had broken completely with John Chapman – a thing which she very rarely did – for she once told Barbara that she felt it wrong even to speak of the shortcomings of anyone she called a friend (*Haight*, v. 123).

13 Better known under her married name. Her biography was written by Evelyn Sharp, *Hertha Ayrton* (London, 1926).

14 One of the first women members of Parliament, Hertha Ayrton's daughter, Barbara Ayrton Gould, as a child consoled her godmother.

15 H. Burton, *Barbara Bodichon* (1949), pp. 182–4.

The New Woman in Drama

IV.

Paris in the Bernhardt Era

At the service of thanksgiving for 'the greatest actress whom I have called friend' – Edith Evans – her biographer told how he, seeing that she was rapidly failing, took aside his little daughter and prepared her by telling her that Dame Edith was very old and was going to die. The child paused in deep thought, then confidently replied, 'No, I don't think she's going to die. She's not the sort!'

Sarah Bernhardt's words to Ellen Terry, 'There are two people who will never be old. You and I, darling', were echoed when Maurice Rostand wrote her epitaph

> Ci-gît Sarah
> Qui survivra.

Sarah Bernhardt, like Edith Evans, was not classically beautiful; the stage self is something that comes when their craftsmanship, so exact and scrupulous, flowers; and 'the god was there', as Sarah said. They served.

> I know what wages beauty gives
> How hard a life her servant lives,

sang Yeats, who fell in love with beauty, and married a plain woman. Even Sarah's detractors conceded that she knew her craft. It seems to me that before great playwrights can make their innovations there must be a high level of craftsmanship among the actors of the 'painted scene'. Those geniuses of the theatre, Shakespeare, Molière, Ibsen, were all craftsmen themselves, but they needed acting material to build on. The actor's art survives on stage.

Throughout the nineteenth century the dominance of Europe – indeed the world – by the Parisian theatre meant that at Paris the great practical experiments were initiated. Playwrights sent their work to Paris, from whence it travelled on to the rest of the world;

Paris was the manufacturing centre. The nineteenth century saw the arrival of international theatre, as the old national traditions merged. Up to then, the ancient centres of theatre in Europe – Paris and London, Italy and Spain – had developed in relative independence their individual styles. The Comédie Française, the Theatre of Molière, safeguarded the French classical tradition by its monopoly of performance. Italy, home of the most continuous formalist tradition, of the *commedia dell'arte*, carnival and marionettes, made its contribution in the form of opera. England's great Shakespearean tradition existed alongside historical spectacular dramas, based largely on Walter Scott; burlesque and pantomime offered a form of entertainment which, even in a Puritan society, Tories could accept; this culminated in Gilbert and Sullivan's operas, the most successful venture of the later Victorian period. After the Lyceum triumphs of Henry Irving and Ellen Terry came the polemical theatre of Shaw and, in the late 1890s, the beginnings of Irish drama at the Abbey Theatre.

To track the French influence would entail a survey of every European capital and parts of the near East also, for it was Napoleon's invasion of Egypt that evoked the first tentative drama in Cairo and Beirut. Like other actresses, Sarah Bernhardt visited Egypt; but all round the perimeter of French hegemony, the French model prevailed in theatres, whilst from the perimeter appeared the new dramatists who were to transform the theatres they served. Great men came from little countries – Norway, Sweden, Ireland – and brought their plays to Paris before they could be more widely known. Ibsen, Strindberg and, of course, Turgenev had to be given in translation; in France, Hauptmann and Suderman were played in French. Wherever Bernhardt played, it was in the tongue of Racine and of Sardou.

The three phases of development on the French stage might be summarised as the advent of a Romantic freedom, of which the *Bataille d'Hernani* in 1830 was the symbol; the gradual growth of contemporary 'realism' during the Second Empire, with Montigny as director, Augier as dramatist; the advent of naturalism in the mid-1880s, and later of symbolism (Théâtre Libre, 1887; Théâtre de l'Oeuvre, 1895).

At the age of twenty-five, Sarah enjoyed her first dazzling success in *Le Passant* of Coppée, whilst in the same year (1869), at the age of forty-one, Ibsen produced his first realist drama, *The League of Youth*, and attended the opening of the Suez Canal. For Sarah, as for Ibsen, the 1860s had provided the 'run-up'; the 1870s brought achievement, culminating at the end of that decade. In 1879 Sarah Bernhardt, with her first visit to London, broke with the Comédie

Française; and began that international career which was to liberate her from French theatrical tradition, and to break up the old repertory system in favour of the 'star vehicle' spectacularly produced. The same year, with the appearance of *A Doll's House*, Ibsen inaugurated the drama of the modern age.

The 1880s saw the consequences of these two events. In 1880 Sarah went to New York, where her most famous role, *La Dame aux Camélias*, was played and in the course of her tour, repeated sixty-five times. Sarah *was* Marguerite Gautier, the victimised and virtuous courtesan; Adrienne Lecouvreur was another such role, but historically distanced. Hereafter increasingly she appeared in plays written specifically for her, mainly by Sardou, though she also tried her own hand at composition. Through the 1880s she alternated foreign tours with Parisian triumphs. The counter-move began in the little amateur theatres; by 1888 Paris had seen *Ghosts*, and the Meininger troupe had paid a visit. *Ghosts* and, in 1890, *The Wild Duck*, did not succeed yet soon Lugné-Poë was staging Strindberg's *Lady Julie* and Hauptmann's *The Weavers* (both 1892), followed by *The Father* (1895).

From world tours (her special trains symbolised the age of new communication), Sarah moved into management (financed by her foreign earnings), first in the theatres run by her son Maurice, then in 1899 at the Théâtre Sarah Bernhardt.

By this time the Théâtre de l'Oeuvre had inaugurated the new wave of the symbolists. Whilst Sarah had acquired a new Romantic poet, Rostand, who supplied her latest famous roles in his plays *Cyrano de Bergerac* and *L'Aiglon* (1900), Maeterlinck was supplying puppet plays for the *avant-garde* theatre of Paris (in 1905 Sarah was to play Pelléas in *Pelléas et Mélisande*). She once (1905) essayed the part of Ellida in *The Lady from the Sea* also; it was not a success, although it had been a triumph for the Théâtre des Escholiers. But what matter if the *avant-garde* production of *An Enemy of the People* was taken as an image of the Dreyfus affair? There was room for more than one theatrical tradition in Paris, and indeed before the end of the century some of the *avant-garde* were writing for the Comédie Française. By 1900, however, the separate establishments of the classical theatre, the popular theatre and the *avant-garde* stage had each its well-defined clientele. If France, the most powerful theatre centre, had expanded its eclecticism to produce plays in other national traditions (in itself an important change) yet these had gained recognition only by the lead given in Paris. Plays were imported, but theatre exported.

Paris still experiments – the ruinous theatre, open to the sky, where Peter Brook furnished his stage with bits of old junk, represented the *avant-garde* of the 1970s. Nowadays if there is no such absolute French predominence, the group of writers drawn from all countries who led the revival of the 1950s resided in Paris – the Irishman Beckett, the Romanian Ionesco, the Russian Adamov, the Spaniard Arrabal.

* * *

For the stage and for her public life Sarah developed both a self and an anti-self. Some years ago *The Three Faces of Eve* presented in a case of split personality the initial face of a very meek, good, compliant little girl out of whom burst an unruly, boisterous tomboy with delinquent tendencies. The mature person who integrated and supplanted both was occasionally troubled by the resurfacing of one or other of the previous selves.

Sarah's style was refined and elegant, her golden voice – so christened by Hugo at the hundredth performance of *Ruy Blas* – a soprano, whose effects were lyric; a very rapid recitative interspersed with her *cri sauvage*. The delicate pathos of her instrument, which at first suited the roles of *jeune princesse* – Monime or Aricie – later displayed a use of the vibrato which her arch-enemy, Shaw, compared to the organ's *voix céleste*. She played boy's parts also. In the role of the victimised lover – Marguerite, Adrienne Lecouvreur, and the rest – the plangency grew till even Andromaque and Athalie became seductive. But she had, of course, been trained in declamation at the Conservatoire as she describes in her *Art du Théâtre*, being taught by Provost, Samson and Regnier. The last was her most admired master. In gesture, however, from the first she showed herself an innovator and she recounts her altercation with her professor about the right, in a very minor role, to turn her back upon the audience:

> Mademoiselle, it is disrespectful of you to turn your back upon the audience . . . But, sir, I was accompanying an old woman to the rear door, and I could not very well escort her backwards . . . Your predecessors, Mademoiselle, whose talents were equal, if not superior to yours, have managed to walk upstage without turning their backs to the audience . . . As he angrily turned to leave, I wasted no time in stopping him. Excuse me, sir, do you think you can reach that door without turning your back to me? . . . He attempted to do so, but then left in a violent temper, turning his back and slamming the door.[1]

The 'theatre of Molière' held her only for a year. As Sarah left the Comédie (after, as a mere student, slapping the face of the leading lady) she developed her art in the freer theatre of the boulevards. Her most celebrated piece of choreography was the death scene in *La Dame aux Camélias* (although all her death scenes became celebrated, and she was required to die in every play). In seduction scenes she used her whole body in a manner as compelling as it was unclassical; she was also a mistress of attitudes, discoveries, as the famous painting by Clairon testifies.

Off-stage she was demonic, flamboyant, and subject to such alarming rages as the one which caused her to horsewhip the woman who had libelled her as Sarah Barnum. She terrified her managers by venturing out on to the ice floes of the St Lawrence River at Montreal. Her vitality drove her to live round the clock, exhausting all her colleagues; she delighted in shooting, in keeping a menagerie of wild animals. She ventured boldly into the arts of painting and sculpture, as well as play writing.

Yet on the stage she was plaintive, elegant, mournful, and wholly feminine, though also essaying transvestite roles. Physically, in some respects, she was frail. She suffered from stage nerves. But when in 1872 she re-entered the Comédie Française as Chimène, Théodore de Banville wrote:

> Very tall, thin, [actually she was *not* tall], endowed with that slimness which we find in so many theatrical heroines, even though it gives such ready ammunition to wit, Mlle Sarah has one of those expressive yet delicate heads that medieval artists painted . . . From Provost she learnt pure, elegant, scrupulously exact diction, but nature gave her a far rarer gift – the quality of being totally and unconsciously lyrical in whatever she attempted. Her voice captures the rhythm and music of poetry as natural-ly as a lyre . . . this makes her quite the opposite of other actors and actresses. They, as Talma so rightly explained, are always troubled by poetry, which locks them in an inexorable bond of words. They are at their best when they obtain the sort of scripts which they can turn to their own ends, a play with lively and well developed situations, in which the style is of no importance . . . Mlle Sarah on the other hand receives all her inspiration and force from poetry, and the nearer she approaches the purely lyrical, the greater she is and the more she is herself. Make no mistake, the engagement of Mlle Sarah Bernhardt at the Comédie Fran-çaise is serious and violently revolutionary. It is poetry entering the realm of dramatic art; it is the wolf in the sheepfold.[2]

When after eight years she resigned for a second time from the Comédie Française, Sarah moved towards just the sort of plays de Banville had rejected for her. Scribe supplied her with *Adrienne Lecouvreur*, the opening play of her New York visit. *Frou Frou* was less tragedy than a fashion show, and the strong melodramas which Sardou wrote for her from 1881 (the date of *Fédora*), with their profusion of jewels, crowds and historic depiction of exotic times and places were combined with the pathos of the virtuous courtesan, with violent deaths, with tortures and triumphs.

Perhaps without the undeviating standards of the Comédie Fran-çaise there would have been nothing to rebel against, nothing to test the muscles. It is still possible for the older classical roles to be transformed, as for instance Hecht transformed the role of Néron in *Britannicus*.

The London public was unprepared for Sarah's combination of delicate lyricism and erotic boldness. One reviewer spoke of her 'orchidaceous air', Matthew Arnold of 'a fugitive vision of delicate features under a shower of hair and a cloud of lace'. As she first landed at Folkestone quay, a young actor, Johnston Forbes Robertson, presented her with a modest bunch of violets; but Oscar Wilde carpeted her path with lilies. Later she studied the part of his *Salome*, which the censor refused to license, and once he said: 'The three women I have admired most in my life are Sarah Bernhardt, Queen Victoria and Lily Langtry. I would have married any one of them.' The first two had in common at least a golden voice – the most outstanding charm of the Queen as of the actress.

According to some, the endless tours caused a hardening of Sarah's style; playing to audiences who could not understand her speech must have had an effect on gesture and led her to spectacle. Sardou, it is said, perfected the clockwork play; he was 'a mere set of fingers with the theatre at the tips of them'.

*   *   *

The apex of Sarah's classical reputation came between 1869, when she achieved her first great success as Zelotto (a transvestite part) in *Le Passant*, and her departure on her first world tour in 1880. The theatrical-spectacular years that followed, the years of Fédora, Théodora, La Tosca, Cléopatre, Gismonde, La Sorcière, coincided with the arrival of the naturalist and then the symbolist theatres. The prophet of the naturalists was Zola, who declared that art should aspire to the condition of journalism. The real furniture, real trees, real rabbits and even real Sèvres china, introduced by Augier at the beginning of the Second Empire gave way to *A Doll's House*, then to the Théâtre Libre (1886) and, in less than a decade, to Strindberg's *Lady Julie* (1888).

The foremost of the English Ibsenites, Bernard Shaw, consistently mocked with deadly praise the art of Sarah Bernhardt, as part of the attack on what he termed Sardoodledom. In the *Saturday Review*, 1 June 1895, he nostalgically recalled the Sarah who had not sold out 'to a high modern development of the circus and the waxworks',

> I confess I regard with a certain jealousy the extent to which this ex-artist, having deliberately exercised her unquestioned right to step down from the national theatre in which she became famous, to posture in a travelling show, is still permitted the privileges and courtesies appertaining to her former rank ... Miss Bernhardt has elected to go round the world pretending to kill people with hatchets and hairpins and making, I

presume, heaps of money. I wish her every success, but I certainly shall not treat her as an artist of the first rank unless she pays me well for it. As a self-respecting critic, I decline to be bought for nothing.[3]

A fortnight later, comparing her with Duse, even more maliciously he links the art of her excessive make-up with her cult of fine art.

> Her dresses and diamonds, if not exactly splendid, are at least splendacious; her figure, far too scantily upholstered in the old days, is at its best; and her complexion shows that she has not studied modern art in vain. Those charming rosette effects which French painters produce by giving flesh the pretty colours of strawberries and cream and painting the shadows pink and crimson are cunningly reproduced by Miss Bernhardt in the living picture. She paints her ears crimson and allows them to peep enchantingly through a few loose braids of her auburn hair. Every dimple has its dab of pink; and her finger tips are so delicately encarnadined that you fancy they are transparent like her ears, and that the light is showing through their delicate blood vessels. Her lips are like a newly-painted pillar box and her cheeks right up to the languid lashes have the bloom and surface of a peach. She is beautiful with the beauty of her school – and entirely inhuman and incredible . . . She adds to her own piquancy by looking you straight in the eye and saying in effect; 'Now who would ever dream that I am a grandmother?'[4]

Shaw did not spare the golden voice his damning praise, as her recitative, 'monotonous chanting on one note', was compared with Duse who 'immeasurably dwarfs the poor little octave and a half on which Sarah Bernhardt plays such pretty canzonets and stirring marches'. Again, comparing hers with Duse's interpretation, 'The coaxing suits well with her acting, which is not the art of making you think more highly or feel more deeply, but the art of making you admire her, champion her, weep with her, laugh at her jokes, follow her fortunes breathlessly and applaud her wildly when the curtain falls.'[5] In 'Sardoodledom' he said of *Fédora* ('one of the claptraps which Sardou contrives for her') that it offers 'the whole Bernhardtian range of sensational effects . . . effects so enormously popular and lucrative that, though their production is hardly more of a fine art than lion-taming, few women who are able for them can resist the temptation to devote their whole lives to them.'

There is no doubt that Shaw himself was the most thorough-going showman and lion-tamer; he resented in Sarah arts which in his own fashion he cultivated. It was his habit to attack the favourite of the hour, a publicity stunt which by now is well attested, if the attacker has sufficient talent. When the Théâtre Libre came to London Shaw attacked the leading actress for playing Rebecca 'à la Bernhardt'.[6]

Yet Sarah was to essay Hamlet; and l'Aiglon, her 'white Hamlet', represented her genuine patriotism, often displayed in ordinary life, from the hospital at l'Odéon, during the Siege of Paris, to the melodramatic pieces of the First World War. Her boyish pathos in l'Aiglon combined with the spirit that had led her on her first international campaign for French theatre (as she explained in her old age to her grand-daughter).

* * *

The development of the French *avant-garde* theatre in the last two decades of the nineteenth century is one of the most well documented subjects in theatrical history. Antoine's acting team was not gifted, but his method was copied. The talented actor Lugné-Poë had indeed opened an amateur theatre before Antoine, and at his Théâtre de l'Art had played *The Cenci*; Mallarmé, Verlaine and others supported him in his reaction against the Théâtre Libre. At his new Théâtre de l'Oeuvre settings were sparse, movements evocative, costumes unrealistic. A marionette *Tempest*, Marlowe and Ford represented the exotically antique, but reacted in favour of the playwright against the absolute predominance of the star.

Shaw had summed up the view of many playwrights when he declared that Sarah substituted personality for characterisation. 'She does not enter into the leading character, she substitutes herself for it.' If she grounded her emotions in technique, Sarah was, in Jouvet's terms, an *actrice* not a *comédienne*, whereas Lugné-Poë subjected himself to the rich, varied material which such playwrights as Ibsen and Strindberg were supplying.

For these playwrights, the Paris stage remained an ideal. In *Ghosts* (1884) Ibsen represented the city as the home of all joy and artistic freedom and of perfect purity to boot. The hero, Osvald, returning to his gloomy Northern fjord describes that artist's life there to his mother and her pastor. The young artist 'can't afford to get married' but lives in a 'proper and comfortable home' in complete decorum 'with his children and his children's mother'. Only model husbands and fathers, in Paris for a spree, 'were able to tell us of places and things we'd never dreamed of'. For bachelors the models ('There are plenty of fine types among the models which you wouldn't see up here') came of an evening to partake of a slice of ham and a bottle of wine before beginning to dance.

Ibsen, in spite of his emancipated views, was extremely Puritan (Strindberg was to term him 'the celebrated Norwegian male bluestocking') and himself did not visit Paris. He allows a vigorous girl like Régine to dream of it, the equally vigorous and ruthless Rita to offer her Alfred 'champagne' with pink lighting. By 1899, in his last play, Irene has posed as a model, naked, on a turntable, evidently in some kind of show. She has travelled all over the world, and claims to have killed her husband with a pin from her hair. The hero regrets not having seduced her when young.

By the time Ibsen wrote this play, the 'new wave' which he had started with *A Doll's House* was succeeded by a third wave; Strindberg was parodying Ibsen, and whilst Shaw was still learning from the naturalism of Brieux (translated into English by Mrs Shaw), the two lines of development had separated. The varied drama of the twentieth century descends from both. Ibsen's world became that of the German naturalists, who went on to contribute to the next great movement, the expressionism of Kaiser and Toller. The 'world within' descended through the later plays of Strindberg and through Pirandello to the modern theatre of the absurd. Polarised, the two produced Beckett at one point, Brecht at the other.

The playwrights had certainly taken the initiative over from the players. That Ibsen had learnt his craftsmanship in the theatres of Norway, dominated by France through Copenhagen, and given to the works of Scribe, provided him with a training that he exercised far from the living stage; but Strindberg married an actress, and after the calamitous break with her, came to Paris where his plays had already been staged. He resided there during the years 1894–6. In Sweden his works were banned but, although the shadows of his 'Inferno' crisis were closing on him, in France he enjoyed success, and this he dramatised in a play set in Paris, *Crimes and Crimes* (1899). It deals with a young playwright whose new drama has made him the toast of the city but who, drawn into a love affair with a beautiful sculptress, Henriette, leaves his mistress Jeanne and their child Marion. He is even heard to say it would be better if the child had not been born; shortly after she dies, and he is suspected of killing her. Although found innocent, he still feels remorse for 'the murder in the heart', and confesses himself to an old Abbé. He goes back to the theatre, absolved.

The setting in Paris is unusually precise for Strindberg; the beautiful cemetery at Montparnasse where Jeanne is chilled by foreboding, recalls Strindberg's actual encounter with a woman mourner in this place. The story is a reflection as always of his own inner conflicts, but in spite of the elements of fantasy, Paris gave Strindberg the impulse for his most 'theatrical' play. He is said too to have met Bernhardt herself in the Montparnasse cemetery, where they engaged in some spiritualist experiments.

With the plays of Strindberg and others, the Paris theatre began to reflect a surrealist view of drama before the end of the century. Twenty years before Dada, Alfred Jarry's plays were staged by Lugné-Poë, and with his work this survey may conclude. What Sarah would have thought of it defies comment. Although she expressed goodwill towards the Théâtre Libre, on Jarry she might have pulled a gun. But on 11 December 1896 she had just enjoyed her great Day of Glorification and was otherwise occupied.

On 10 December Sardou, Coppée, Rostand, Jules Lemaître and others organised a day of tribute, beginning with a banquet in the Salle du Zodiac of the Grand Hotel. Five hundred guests gathered for lunch, a theatre ticket, a medal and a Golden Book of the Gala. Sarah appeared on a balcony in a white dress embroidered in gold and trimmed with sable. It was reported that as she descended

> Her long train followed her like a graceful tame serpent. At every turn she bent over the railing and twined her arms like an ivy wreath round the velvet pillars whilst she acknowledged the acclamations with her disengaged hand. Her lithe and slender body scarcely seemed to touch the earth. She was wafted towards us in a halo of glory.

For the feast she sat between the Minister of Fine Arts and the personal representative of the President of the Republic. Afterwards the star appeared in the third act of *Phèdre* and the fourth of *Rome Vaincue*; then was staged the Apotheosis of Sarah Bernhardt. The poets came on to read their tributes. Rostand opened as follows:

> En ce temps sans beauté, seule tu encore nous restes,
> Sachant descendre, pale, un grand escalier clair,
> Ceindre un bandeau, prêtre un lys, brandir un fer,
> Reine de l'attitude et princesse des gestes.

At the end Sarah dissolved in tears, whilst showers of camellias rained down on her from the flies.[7]

At the other end of the spectrum, on the following night, history was being made in the Théâtre de l'Oeuvre. The past and future touched each other here; this sustaining relationship makes the story of Sarah Bernhardt part of the continuing life of the theatre, and ensures that she survives through the living currents of the actor's art.

10 and 11 December 1896 epitomised the struggle between the theatre of the star-actor and the theatre of the poets. Whether playing the great classic roles — Sarah was always comparing herself with Rachel — or the made-to-measure part of a spectacular melodrama, the actor resisted the new theatre until it had become more familiar. The *avant-garde* theatre was the counter-assertion of the writer; if Sarah reduced the playwright to a puppeteer, Jarry reduced the actor to a puppet. His *Ubu-Roi* was closely based on Shakespeare's *Hamlet* — which Sarah was to play — indeed the author claims Ubu turns into Shakespeare:

> Then Father Ubu shakes his speare, who was afterwards yclept Shakespeare by the English, and you have from under his own hand many lovely tragedies by this name.

11 December, the opening night of *Ubu Roi,* saw one of the great French theatrical riots – perhaps the most significant since the *Bataille d' Hernani.* Again it was the language that roused the audience – the curtain rose on Ubu's cry of 'Merdre!' Among the crowd were W. B. Yeats and Arthur Symons. Yeats wrote,

> I go to the first performance of Jarry's *Ubu Roi* . . . The audience shake their fists at one another and my friend whispers to me 'There are often duels after these performances', and he explains to me what is happening on the stage. The players are supposed to be toys, dolls, marionettes, and now they are all hopping like wooden frogs, and I can see for myself that the chief personage, who is some kind of King, carries for Sceptre a brush of the kind we use to clean a closet. Feeling bound to support the most spirited party, we have shouted for the play but that night at the Hôtel Corneille, I am very sad, for comedy, objectivity, has displayed its growing power once more. I say 'After Stephane Mallarmé, after Paul Verlaine, after Gustave Moreau, after Puvis de Chavannes, after our own verse, after all our subtle colour and nervous rhythm, after the faint mixed tints of Corot, what more is possible? After us, the Savage God?[8]

As it happened, Mallarmé approved. Symons describes the painted scene, representing both indoors and outdoors, even the torrid and arctic zones simultaneously. At the foot of a bed stood a tree, snow-laden; there were also palm trees, a boa constrictor, a gallows with pendant skeleton. Changes of scene were announced by placards. Among the artists cited as inspiration was Gauguin.

Here is the polarisation of Sarah's theatre, but the French theatre was strong enough to tolerate these opposites; indeed, only in so strong a setting could they appear. Revolt did not induce collapse – only counter-movements. Contraries are more positive than mere negation; the *avant-garde* theatre was sustained by the opposing power of the establishment. Together they provided a force that held society magnetised. True classicism is that which can tolerate change, and without changing its identity, can modify itself to accommodate the new works. This kind of confidence gave to the French theatre the power to radiate its art, as well as absorb changes.

So, a week after witnessing the Ubu riot, Yeats met the shy young student who lived on the top floor of the Hotel Corneille, and invited John Millington Synge to come back to Ireland. From that encounter on 16 December came Synge's new life on Aran, his one fine tragedy, the kind of comedy that in a few years produced riots in Dublin. He fell in love with an actress, and died at the height of his powers, leaving a legend to the Abbey. To that legend, France had contributed.

Notes

1 *L'art du théâtre*, pp. 123–4, quoted from Gerda Taranow, *Sara Bernhardt, the Art within the Legend* (Princeton, 1972), p. 98, the best account of Sarah's acting technique.
2 *Critiques* (Paris, 1917) pp. 370–2, quoted from Marvin Carlson, *The French Stage in the Nineteenth Century* (New Jersey, The Scarecrow Press, 1972), pp. 151–2.
3 G. Bernard Shaw, *Our Theatre in the Nineties* (Constable, 1912), pp. 137–8.
4 ibid., pp. 149.
5 ibid., p. 150.
6 ibid., p. 74.
7 See Cornelia Otis Skinner, *Madame Sarah* (The Riverside Press, 1966), pp. 255–8.
8 W. B. Yeats, *Autobiographies* (Macmillan & Co., 1958), pp. 23–4.

V.
A Doll's House and the Unweaving of the Web

At Christmas 1879 – though not quite immediately – the appearance of *A Doll's House* brought the fame of Henrik Ibsen to England. The social emancipation of women, especially through literary women, had been established a generation earlier; in 1845 Elizabeth Barrett Browning had eloped to Italy, and George Eliot, who had gone abroad in 1854 to live with G. H. Lewes, was, by the end of the 1870s, a venerated figure. In this year, 1879, Sarah Bernhardt came to London, having walked out of the Comédie Française and slammed the door.

But in the preliminary notes for his play Ibsen had set forward a position so radical that it might well be used today as a feminist manifesto:

> There are two kinds of moral law, two kinds of conscience, one in man, and a completely different one in woman. They do not understand each other; but in matters of practical living the woman is judged by a man's law, as if she were not a woman but a man . . . A woman cannot be herself in contemporary society, it is an exclusively male society, with laws drafted by men, and with counsel and judges who judge feminine conduct from the masculine point of view . . . She has committed a crime and is proud of it because she did it for love of her husband and to save his life . . . Now and then like a woman, she shrugs off her thoughts. Sudden return of dread and terror. Everything must be borne alone.

However, at the end of the 'Ibsen decade' (the 1880s) when the play had appeared in London, Milan, Paris and Budapest Ibsen told the Society for Extended Female Education in Vienna, in 1891, that it was not about women's rights but the rights of humanity in general; in 1898 he repeated this to the Norwegian Women's Rights League ('What courage!' observed Nigel Dennis), adding 'I am not even quite sure what women's rights are' (Meyer, *Henrik Ibsen* (1971), 3, pp. 177, 297).

In the terms of a later generation his interests were psychological rather than sociological; he said he did not believe in 'external revolutions'; the revolution 'must come from within'.

Ibsen's work made its effect in translation into languages he did not always understand; it was read much more than performed.[1] Today it survives because of its power in performance. Modern rediscovery of Ibsen followed the stage and broadcast revivals of the 1950s. The full impact of this play survives across language barriers because Ibsen has employed all the arts of the theatre. Perhaps because the theatre in which he was trained had relied on translations for most of its performances and had little of its own, Ibsen succeeded in developing (at the age of fifty-one and in his fifteenth play) a reticulation or meshing of human relationships which elastically adapts itself in live action; the space between the characters, the links that divide and unite them, the space between actors and audience, and the flow of empathy that sustains performance, each derives from Ibsen's employment of all the kinds of communication possible in drama. Words and sub-text, the setting and the invisible, eliminated or superseded drafts upon which Ibsen worked forward to his final form supply a 'complex variable' capable of all the modulations recently chronicled in Daniel Haakonsen's *Henrik Ibsen, mennesket og kunstneren* (Oslo, 1981).

The original Nora, Betty Hennings, had begun her career as a ballerina; one of Ibsen's final inspirations, Nora's tarantella, embodies the heroine's terror and despair, while concentrating her power as Eve, the prime delight and temptress of men. Like the dance of Anitra in *Peer Gynt*, the dance of the Capri fishergirl belongs to an untamed Southern scene, but it has now been transported from Egypt to the cosy little home with its stove, draped table and upright piano, from which the dancer will depart into a Norwegian night.

The delicious life-giving power radiating from Nora must be controlled and kept jealously for her male circle: 'You and papa have done me a grave wrong', she finally tells her husband. Nora's forging of her dying father's signature has outraged her husband equally as a lawyer and as President of the Bank; but to her the gold of his wedding ring has become a bigger fraud, since the President is found to be spiritually bankrupt, totally self-deceived.

Livsglaeden, that untranslateable word, the fountain of life, dances in the faded images of the little skylark, the little squirrel; an actress can still embody it. Nowhere else in Ibsen do the lineaments of animal desire show as plainly as in Torvald Helmer's 'Don't want to? don't want to? aren't I your husband?' Payment on the nail is the protector's right; it is no 'demand of the ideal'.

Whatever harsh privation his new urban environment inflicted on man's primal energies, the child-wife and father-husband relation, that popular model for happy marriages in the mid-nineteenth century, immensely fortified the home as enclosure, cradle and prison. The skylark, the pet squirrel plays in a cage. At the end, Torvald's magnanimous act of forgiving his wife leaves her in exactly the position that he had seen as being his own under the blackmailer's power:

> Here I am, in the grip of a man without a conscience; he can do whatever he likes with me, demand anything he wants, order me about just as he chooses . . . and I daren't breathe a word.

The happy state of affairs to which Torvald later looks forward was a sort of spiritual cannibalism: 'Open your whole heart to me, and I shall become both your will-power and your conscience.' At the beginning, he had been forbidding his baby doll to eat macaroons or do mending in the drawing-room; he kept the key of the letter-box in his pocket, and when Nora inadvertently let slip a word of criticism, he straightway asserted his authority over her by dispatching Krogstad's letter of dismissal. For once he and Krogstad agree as lawyers in thinking that Nora's disappearance or suicide would not absolve him from possible accusations of having instigated her forgery. Nora's rejection of his sexual approach is dismissed with 'What's this? You've played the fool with me long enough, little Nora.' Finally, he opens her last letter from Krogstad, refusing to give it her. Her childish pet name (she was christened Eleanora, as Ibsen explained to his family, who gave that name to his grand-daughter) means that to translate 'Nora', something like 'Nolly-dolly' is needed.

The eternal child-wife must remain unconscious of the sexual implications of her own pretty games whilst she daydreams about legacies from elderly admirers. She is expert at undressing herself in imagination for Dr Rank. She dresses up and plays parts for Torvald almost like Harold Pinter's girls. In Ibsen's first draft she reveals that her father liked her to write poetry and learn French, but Torvald preferred dramatic recitations, and disapproved of French literature; his own fantasies of secret mistresses and bridal nights, revealed in his cups, come out of cheap novelettes. Dr Rank slips into calling her 'Nora' but the truly familiar 'du' is reserved for the men between each other, the two women together, and the husband and wife; three different linkings of the threads. Inside 'Nolly-dolly' another self is growing up. She may enjoy playing at secrets, the secrets of the Christmas tree; but her copying work (in the first draft *not* a secret from Torvald) makes her feel 'almost like a man'; and at the news of

Torvald's power to dismiss such bank employees as Krogstad, she feels an impulse to swear.

The audience is never told of the emergent adult growing in the chrysalis of the doll's house; they are left to fill her in, or fill her out. Her unconscious growth towards maturity is accompanied by self-delusive dreams of Torvald, the chivalrous knight-errant; and by blank disregard for the concerns of others. When her instinct to love and cherish is in collision with brute facts, she cannot bear to hurt, and would rather lie. She is not alone in this.

> There wasn't the slightest chance that they could go to the lighthouse tomorrow, Mr Ramsay snapped out irascibly.
>
> How did he know? she asked. The wind often changed. The extraordinary irrationality of her remark, the folly of women's minds enraged him. She flew in the face of facts, made his children hope what was utterly out of the question, in effect, told lies. He stamped his foot on the stone 'Damn you' he said . . . To pursue truth with such astonishing lack of consideration for other people's feelings, to rend the thin veils of civilisation so wantonly, so brutally, was to her so horrible an outrage of human decency that, without replying, dazed and blinded, she bent her head as if to let the pelt of jagged hail, the drench of dirty water, batter her unrebuked. There was nothing left to be said. (Virginia Woolf, *To the Lighthouse* (Everyman edn, pp. 36–7))

Nora begs Krogstad to think of her children, and his reply 'Did you or your husband think of mine?' is quite as devastating as Torvald's 'I am saved, Nora, I am saved', when he finds the fatal IOU has been returned. (In the first draft he says 'We are saved'.)

In a letter to Brandes, written as early as 1871, Ibsen had described the scientists and artists of every age as showing a family likeness – the artist possessing as instinct or intuition what the scientist learnt as knowledge (Meyer, 2, p. 148). In the psychology of everyday life Ibsen and Strindberg anticipated Freud, who was himself later to comment on the 'case' of Rebekka West.[2]

Since *A Doll's House* is not psychiatry but drama, the whole plot is woven in a network of relationships. The characters are symbiotically linked so that the minor figures supply a 'feed' to the main figures at a much deeper level than that of the narrative.

Rank and Krogstad are both old school friends of Torvald, Kristine of Nora; each presents a shadow side of the twin. The cross-relationships become a closed system. We do not know what Torvald's chief clerk is like, the details of Rank's practice were suppressed; we do not know whether Nora's childbirths were hard or easy, or what was the character of Krogstad's first wife. But we know that Kristine has been forced by necessity to develop her masculine qualities, to become a breadwinner (also, earlier, to sell herself in the marriage-market). The hard, cold insight which makes her tell Krogstad she won't resign the job at the bank in which she has displaced him 'for that wouldn't help you at all' created what is eventually Nora's equally hard, cold insight into her own situation. Kristine deliberately stops Krogstad from claiming back his letter of disclosure; replacing Dr Rank as ruthless experimenter, she detonates the explosion. Yet Kristine herself is hungry for a home, hungry to be needed, as Nora is hungry for freedom. She had long ago broken Krogstad as Nora breaks Torvald ('I felt as though the ground were cut from under my feet') but now the family for whom she sacrificed herself are no longer in need of her, she feels desolate and empty. In the first draft she was still supporting her brothers; this detracts from her egoistic energy, as she greets the future in words that anticipate Nora's. Tidying up a little, and putting ready her outdoor clothes, to meet Krogstad who is waiting below:

> What a change! O what a change! [literally a turning in the road]. People to work for – people to live for. A home that needs to *feel* like home! Well, now I'll set to, straight away. [In the first draft, 'We'll set to'] . . . I wish they'd hurry! Ah, there they are! Get my things.

But the competent Kristine radiates from no fountain of life; 'she's a bore, that woman', says Torvald. Malice would recall the epigram 'She lives for others. You can tell the others by the hunted look in their eyes.' When Nora comes in after putting off her fancy dress, Torvald cries 'What's this? Not going to bed? You've changed?', and she replies 'Yes, Torvald, I've changed.' There is no verbal echo in the Norwegian, as there is in English, but to dress for a journey links the two scenes dramatically and in action. As Kristine finds a city home, Nora sets out for her birthplace, in search of herself.

In her last speech Nora brings together her whole life, the dead father and her eight years marriage 'with a stranger'[3] so that the past looms into the present at several levels, not only at the one of her dangerous secret. Torvald reproaches her for her ingratitude, and blames himself for having turned advocate for the defence when sent by his ministry to investigate her father's affairs. Ibsen suppressed the passage from the first draft, where he says that he could find no trace of the 1200 dollars her father was supposed to have given her just before his death, for it would be tactless to enquire why Torvald, the lawyer, did not check fully the details of a transaction from which so unexpectedly he had benefited. An audience should not have its notice drawn to the inconsistency. It has rightly been allowed to feel, earlier, that Nora has some basis for her dreams of Torvald's chivalry in the kindness he had shown her 'poor papa'.

As we never hear about anyone outside the charmed circle of

home, so the close detail and meshing of the foreground distinguish *A Doll's House* from its immediate predecessor, *Pillars of the Community* (1877). Here women's rights are shown in a feminine group ranging from the emancipated Lona to the patient Martha, who, like Solveig in *Peer Gynt*, sits at home spinning and waiting for her lover to return. Though Ibsen had begun the art of elimination and of carving in high relief, Bernick's relations with his whole community dominate. (The women do not supply the action of the play.) A large cast of nineteen are found flowing in and out of the garden-room at Bernick's. The irony is far more direct ('Just repaired! and in your own yard, Mr Bernick! . . . now if she's been one of those floating coffins you hear about in the bigger countries!'), and is not so fully integrated with the language of stage movement.

By contrast, Torvald's address to Nora through the half-open door as, unknown to him, she is 'changing', allows him in half-soliloquy to cast himself as a hero, till in his inflation he triumphantly reaches the cheap image of a dove rescued from a hawk – almost becoming something birdlike. The script must be his alone – to her earlier cry 'You mustn't take it on yourself!' he had snapped 'Stop play-acting!' Her language from this moment is naked, plain (in contrast to her horror when Dr Rank spoke out to her of his love). But at the end, when Torvald in a mixture of threat and appeal says 'Then only one explanation is possible . . . you don't love me any more', her simple 'No; that's it. Exactly' brings back the angry cross-examining lawyer: 'Then perhaps you can also explain to me?' In the first draft she had attacked Torvald;[4] in the final version she defines and describes, gives orders to her husband, to which he responds with bewildered questions. The last difficult definition of the 'miracle' that their 'common life' (*samliv*) 'might become a marriage' (*ekteskap*) annihilates Torvald as lawyer and as man.

The word's power is extended in its context.[5] The silences of Dr Rank, his 'Thanks for the light', and the black cross above his name on the visiting card that, according to social ritual, has been dropped, anticipate the depth of Nora's own speech. Her inner death does not leave enough relationship to merit reproaches.

These depths belong with Shakespeare's *Macbeth* and Racine's *Andromaque*. When Lady Macbeth says 'He that's coming/Must be provided for', or Pyrrhus 'Rien ne vous engage à m'aimer en effet', breaking by his obtuseness the barrier of Hermione's control, then a long-built tension explodes; but Ibsen contrives this in the speech of everyday life. (Lady Macbeth is indeed matter of fact, but the context is high poetry.)

In Ibsen's prose the tensions come partly from the relation between the characters, partly from that between his play and what was expected of such dramas (the model of Scribe). On stage the first audience, while enjoying the charm of Nora, actually took Torvald's point of view and thought him a decent husband.[6] In the theatre they followed the familiar code which Ibsen was breaking. It was reading that convinced them of his intention. By the time he had finished drafting and redrafting *A Doll's House* the original notes did not apply, and he was justified in saying it was not a question of women's rights. The tensions come from the marriage between the word and its context, and this works as rhythm works in poetry. But the verse rhythms of Ibsen were very simple; it was only in prose that he gained the classic freedom of his great predecessors.

As he said again and again, his resources were within; he created out of himself, yet he did not subsequently impose an interpretation. He would not tell actors how to play their roles, nor tell the audience how Mrs Alving acted with the morphine: 'That everyone must decide for himself.' The plays grew into contexts he did not know. One translation was called '*Breaking a Butterfly*'. Hauptmann wrote '*Before Sunrise*', and Brieux '*Damaged Goods*' out of *Ghosts*; Shaw put back a lot of theory, and wrote *Candida*.

It is still difficult to accept Ibsen's assertion that he was not depicting Laura Keiler, his disciple, who to take her sick husband to Italy in 1876 had borrowed without his knowledge; and afterwards, when her guarantor fell ill, wrote a poor piece of work which Ibsen refused to recommend to his publisher. It was after this that she desperately forged a cheque; her husband turned on her, tried to take the children and obtain a divorce, for she had collapsed, and put her in a mental hospital with violent patients. Later she went back to him.

On a second occasion Ibsen refused even to make a public denial of any connection between Laura Keiler and his play, when Brandes had launched an attack on her.[7] Since Laura Keiler's story was widely known the general public could not fail to make the connection, although for Ibsen the originating story bore no relation to the work he had made. Ibsen was later to say that he did not depict himself in his plays,[8] disclaiming identification with his 'enemy of the people', Dr Stockmann. He risked even more in the later plays, but these were built on enigmas and paradoxes. In *When We Dead Awake* the sculptor describes how he changed his own work.

Something much nearer Laura Keiler's story (and her feminism) appears in the preliminary notes for what was then termed *A Modern Tragedy*; the germinative process produced something very different. In Mrs Keiler's story there was no Dr Rank, no Krogstad, no Mrs Linde, no dramatic context for the events which made the narrative 'line' into a dramatic web.

The play is not a dramatic monologue for Nora with supporting assistance. The great final scene impresses with its truth, but not as a transcript of anything that could actually happen; it is itself the 'miracle' it postulated. Passions are disentangled from the criss-cross tangles of ordinary life; all the characters being at once so closely enmeshed with each other, yet so isolated from any other crowd or chorus figures, the detail is not realistic.

Ibsen said that as well as character, his people must have a fate. Nora's fate is to embrace an unknown future – to carry the bright flame of her vitality into the dark. 'Out into the storm of life' is one of Borkman's most ironic fantasies; Nora seeks a deep solitude. 'It is necessary that I stand alone.'

'I look into myself; there is my battleground', said Ibsen; his characters say the same:

> Within, within! that is my call
> That is the way I must venture. That is my path.
> One's own innermost heart – *that* is the world.
> (*Brand*, Oxford Ibsen 3, p. 114)
>
> [Innad! innad! Det er ordet!
> Dit gaar veien. Der er sporet!
> Eget hjerte – *det* er kloden.]

The characters of Ibsen's plays stem most clearly from his own innermost heart when he has sometimes to drive out minor, gesticu-latory, symbolic figures who come irrelevantly. In the first draft of *A Doll's House*, Dr Rank talks of a patient, a miner who blew his own right hand off when in drink. Rank may have his special reasons to be hard on this sort of case. (He thinks social care for social failures is turning Norway into a clinic!) The self-mutilated, the murderer in *Brand*, the conscript in *Peer Gynt*, are almost as innocent as the victims in *The Wild Duck* and old Foldal in *John Gabriel Borkman*. Brendel challenges Rebekka to chop off her finger or her ear, Hedda's demands on Løvborg have a squalid sequel. Consul Bernick puts the case of the engineer's need to send a workman to almost certain death. Ibsen killed part of himself. Here, more subtly, Torvald's cruelty is closely linked with squeamishness. The ruthless visionary, the expansive self-intoxicated orator, the down-and-out with visions of grandeur, the doomed child, the woman of narrow aims and iron will, the doctor who judges, are all part of Ibsen's inner society. (Yeats termed his own 'the circus animals'.) Some ghosts found local homes in people Ibsen met, others represent only facets of himself; none is simply repeated. The black comedy or satire from *Pillars of the Community* is concentrated in aspects of Torvald.

Ibsen had freed himself, at the cost of exile, from years of humiliating subservience in theatres at Oslo and Bergen. He had learnt the craft as a junior stage-manager, who also wrote to order: cheap reproductions of Romanticism gave models for his ideals of Norwegian nationalism. His history plays developed a very limited originality, and it was only after eleven years and five plays that he broke free in *Love's Comedy* (1862). Two years later he left for Rome where he wrote *Brand*, declaring the truest form of love is hate.

A Doll's House returns to Norway's urban scene, but also transforms the elements of the well-made plays on which he had toiled so long. It retains old melodramatic tricks, object the sensitive critics of the twentieth century. Rather, it is Sardou *plus*, Scribe *plus*, Ibsen's stagiest work. The characters think they are living in the theatre, they make up cheap plays for themselves but find they are in a different drama. Stage satire does not prevent the use of basic theatrical experience. Ibsen had lived thirteen years in the Norwegian doll's house and written seven plays before he slammed the door.

A Doll's House was composed in Italy where he had gone on his first emancipation – it remained for him the land where feelings were released. The final draft was completed by the sea, always for him a source of primal energies. (For ten years, living in Germany, he had denied himself the sea.) The tarantella of the Capri fishergirl must have come out of his surroundings; he was living in the beautiful little city whence Webster's Duchess of Malfi took her title, but this earlier feminist rebel could not have been known to him.

The successive drafts are Ibsen's substitute for stage rehearsals (which in his day were perfunctory). Today, a director may try out something in rehearsal, only to discard it. Even when a play begins its run considerable modifications to the text, as well as to blocking and presentation, evolve from the effects of full performance. It is not unknown for a whole set to be changed.

If Norway and Scribe had played Torvald to Ibsen's Nora, his exorcism gave him a figure which he grew to know ever more distinctly as an individual. One day he told Susannah, his wife, that he had seen Nora; she came to him and put her hand on his shoulder. Her hands were important (he even broke through his usual amenability to object of one actress that her hands were not right for the part). In an early draft she suddenly sees them as criminal, and shrinks with horror as she decks the Christmas tree ('Not with these hands!'. Her hysteria takes the form of stroking a muff and crying 'Pretty, pretty gloves!'

Ibsen told Susannah that she was wearing a blue woollen dress; blue was his favourite colour. As an old man, he guiltily conspired with his beautiful daughter-in-law, Bergliot, to buy an expensive set of blue velvet curtains for his dreary apartment. (Susannah was conspicuously lacking in the gift of home-making, shared by many of Ibsen's fascinating women.)

Laura Keiler in 1871 had received from Ibsen that telling observation 'Intellectually, man is a long-sighted animal . . . we see most clearly at a distance; details distract; one must remove oneself from what one wants to describe; one describes the summer best on a winter day' (Meyer, 2, p. 125). He continued, 'It is not a matter of willing to go in this direction, but of willing what one absolutely must because one is oneself and cannot do otherwise.'

One sees society best in solitude perhaps. Ibsen's final version, after a long gestation, usually came quickly. After 1877 the regular rhythm evolved of one play every two years, with about two months in late summer and early autumn for the final shaping. It was a natural rhythm, like breathing or sleeping, that came at maturity, at first in a controlled way. Other rhythms, like swimming or riding, often become instinctive with practice.

In his verses 'The Portrait of the Artist at Home', Ibsen described 'his children', his creations dancing round him, living a life of their own, rosy and fresh as if from a bath; if he betrays his presence, the play stops. All theatre – in *A Doll's House* metatheatre also – for him takes the form of a children's game (hide-and-seek). The play had taken hold of him, he accepts its autonomy 'living to live in a world of time beyond me . . . lips parted, the hope, the new ships'. T. S. Eliot's poem about the integration of his own art with that of the past drew from Shakespeare the vision of a girl, a daughter

> What is this face, less clear, and clearer,
> The pulse in the arm, less strong and stronger –
> Given or lent? More distant than stars and nearer than the eye . . .
>   this form, this face, this life
> Living to live in a world of time beyond me.[9]
>
> (*Marina*, 18–20, 30–1)

At the price of deep solitude, total insulation, the liberation of imaginative forms results in an orchestration of their actions which comes from the depths. Ibsen had said '*Brand* began to grow within me like an embryo', but it was at first as a poem, not a drama. The dramatic form suddenly asserted itself. Ibsen was a dramatist as Chopin was a pianist; he could use no other form. But Ibsen wrote concertos and symphonies, not sonatas; he remained free from the actual presence of the theatre, yet clearly bound to it. In the title of *A Doll's House* both his separation from and his ingestion of the theatre where he had learnt his trade is faintly adumbrated; for to look into the peep-show of the nineteenth century's picture-stage is indeed to look into a doll's house (with furniture painted on the backcloth). Not as the result of planning, but of steady, patient work on experience that has been 'lived through' – as he phrased it – the final form emerged; imperative, autonomous, a mimesis that generates new forms of mimesis, with their own life, within the audience and through the years.

Creative opportunities for this third mimesis[10] by the audience are still open. (For example, in this age when racial inequalities have largely replaced sexual inequalities as ground for public concern, the effect of having a white Torvald and a black Nora might be worth some director's experiment.)

The integration of conscious and unconscious functions in the verbal and non-verbal languages of the play generates valid new performance in the live theatre. In a book much studied by Ibsen, it is said of wisdom that 'remaining in herself, she maketh all things new'.

Notes

1 The impact of the stage nevertheless made diction into dynamite. 'It exploded like a bomb', as Halvden Koht remembered from his childhood. In a similar fashion, Synge's *The Playboy of the Western World* was later to enrage the susceptibilities of a Dublin audience. Something of the stage impact may be learnt from Daniel Haakonsen, *Henrik Ibsen, mennesket og kunstneren* (Oslo, 1981) where more than 450 illustrations, including two dozen of 'Nora's dans', may be found.

2 Sigmund Freud, born in Moravia in 1856, went to Paris to study with Charcot in 1885; returning to Vienna he published *Studies in Hysteria* (with Breuer) in 1893, *The Interpretation of Dreams* in 1900 and *Psychopathology of Everyday Life* in 1901. His characteristic work thus came after Ibsen had finished writing. His account of Rebekka as 'the dramatist's conscious creation' points out the relevance of the Oedipus complex both to her desire to supplant Beata, and the horror with which she discovers her truly incestuous past. (See *Ibsen Penguin Critical Anthology*, p. 398.)

3 In real life, Katherine Mansfield was to say 'Perhaps I made Jack up'; in the theatre the most harrowing anticipation is Troilus's 'This is and is not Cressid', as he watches her lovemaking with Diomed. For this use of the past see my 'Ibsen and the Past Imperfect', in *Literature in Action* (1972).

4 'No thanks, no demonstration of affection, not the slightest sign of any thought of saving me. Nothing but reproaches . . . sneers at my father . . . petty little fears . . . bullying and abusing a defenceless victim.' (Tr. McFarlane, *Works* V, p. 341.)

5 The phrase comes from Inga Stina Ewbank, translator of several Ibsen

plays, and the most percipient modern critic of his language.

6 See Frederick and Lise-Lone Marker, 'The first Nora; notes on the world premiere of *A Doll's House*', *Contemporary approaches to Ibsen* (*Ibsen Yearbook* 2, 1970–1, ed. Daniel Haakonsen, Oslo). The first play to give immediate offence in the theatre was *Ghosts*. Strindberg defended both husbands.

7 See B. M. Kinck, 'Henrik Ibsen og Laura Keiler', *Edda* (1935), pp. 504–6. Used by Meyer.

8 A betrothal ring had been cast into the fjord in *Love's Comedy*; but in Ibsen's last play, *When We Dead Awake*, the nude statue of the beloved Irene is named The Resurrection Day.

9 Eliot's girl figures have been identified with various historic women, but, like Ibsen, Eliot always rejected these identifications.

10 The three stages of mimesis are derived from a seminar held by Paul Ricoeur. See *The Rule of Metaphor* (1981).

VI.

'In Dreams Begin Responsibilities'

Naturalism, symbolism, expressionism and futurism swirl through the 'little theatres' in the forty crowded and turbulent years between Strindberg's prosecution for blasphemy in 1884 and the founding of Pirandello's Art Theatre in Rome in 1925. The lands on Europe's periphery – Scandinavia, Ireland, Russia – like Germany and even Italy still took their lead from Paris, which became the dramatists' second home. Turgenev took *A Month in the Country* (1850) from Balzac's *La Marâtre*; it did not appear in St Petersburg till 1879. In the critical years, at the turn of the century, Strindberg lived and set a play in Paris; Synge and Yeats began there, and Pirandello's drama was launched through his friendship with James Joyce.[1]

It is now not obvious that the common theme of women's relationships did not so much reflect sexual freedom as the effect of her individuation upon the family as a whole. Strindberg's first blast of the trumpet against the 'monstrous regiment of women' was entitled *The Father*. Permissiveness towards the flux of attachment need not modify the chieftainship of the family group as Turgenev showed; in *Six Characters in Search of an Author*, Pirandello's father arranges for his supplanter to live with the mother. Through the relationship of man and woman a larger relation with the future as well as with society is mediated; the sexual, and particularly the genital, is the route to acceptance and mastery of the environment.

In Eastern Europe woman became a symbol for the socially subjected, and her role in drama is crucial. Conflict between a powerful matriarch and a dependent young woman is the theme of *A Month in the Country*, and also of Ostrovski's masterpiece, *The Storm* (1860). The German stage of the 1890s was filled with victimised women – who had occupied it since Hebbel's *Maria Magdalena*. At the turn of the century Chekov's three great final plays[2] coinciding with Strindberg's 'second wave' of play writing,

showed women resolutely enduring in the hope of future better-
ment. The one poetic tragedy from Britain in this period, Synge's
peasant story *Riders to the Sea* (1905), culminates in a maternal
lament.

Synge was writing for a nationalist stage where Ireland herself was
personified as a poor old woman. As the twentieth century progres-
sed, the heroic masculine virtues seemed impotent in the face of vast
social sources of oppression. The maternal power of endurance
became *the* heroic virtue for the revolutionary expressionists, whilst
the conscript or the prisoner represented heroism in men; culminating later in Brecht's *Mother Courage*.

* * *

Today, to be prosecuted for blasphemy might be considered the
making of a young dramatist. However in 1884, though acquitted in
court and fêted by the *avant garde*, Strindberg firmly believed that his
real opponents were the feminists and that they had used the pietism
of the Queen as a lever to institute proceedings against his collection
of stories, *Getting Married*, the chief feature of which was an attack
upon Ibsen's *A Doll's House*.

The mocking, high spirited comedy of Strindberg's bash at 'the
celebrated male Norwegian blue-stocking' derives from the breezy
virility of its naval hero, in whose language a fresh wind seems to
blow from the archipelago where his family live, in the officers'
quarters on Long Row; his strength and confidence is echoed from
the bright scene. Sea images give indirect and powerful sexual
reinforcement:

> Cutters came sailing in on the morning breeze, flags fluttered, shots
> crackled, bright summer dresses twinkled on the custom house wharf,
> the steamer with the red water-line came in from Uton, the fishermen
> drew up their nets, and the sun shone on the rippling blue water and the
> green fertile land. (trans. Mary Sandbach, *Getting Married*, 1971, p. 169)

Finding his wife being drawn into Ibsenism by a pious spinsterish
schoolteacher, given *A Doll's House*, and led into parrotting the
language of emancipation, on the advice of his wise mother-in-law,
the naval officer plunges into talk on statistics, which his wife doesn't
understand. He proceeds to flirt with the intruder, sees her home,
kisses her before his wife, who breaks off the connection. Finally,
after he has swept his wife off for a sleigh ride, a party, and a new
seduction, the triumphant strategist invites his mother-in-law for a
visit:

> 'You'll find the dolls dancing, the skylarks and squanderbirds singing and
> twittering, and joy enough to lift the roof off, for no one there is expecting

miracles that happen only in story books. You'll find a real doll's house there, I promise you.' (p. 184)

Later landscapes of Eden, the Fairhaven of *A Dream Play*, the little red house by the shore in the last part of *The Great Highway*, with its orchard and box hedges, share the same doll's house charm with the tiny cottages of Long Row. Strindberg, like Blake, depicted Heaven and Hell as two contrary states of the human soul – he saw the human psyche not only in relation to others but to the whole climate of a world. That world, for him, was a particular Swedish scene.

In turn, for Strindberg, his delicate poetic response to the world of the senses – to scents, touch, sound – was focused through the relation of men and women. He was thirty-five at the time of the prosecution; D. H. Lawrence was not yet born, and Freud was an unknown young doctor studying in Paris with Charcot. He had already anticipated modern theories of the unconscious (indeed, Freud asserted that poets knew it intuitively). In *The Father*, a black, desperate nightmare, there may be some recollection of *The Wild Duck*, and the torturing doubts about the child's paternity,[3] but the bond of negative feelings, the strength of love and hate in conjunction, was banished from consciousness by idealists, radical or conservative. For Strindberg, interpersonal conflict became a source of energy; the beauty of life for him consisted in its cruel struggles. Laura, ironically named after Petrarch's idealised mistress, in her determination to gain sole possession of her child, undermines her husband's confidence in his paternity. Like Shakespeare's *Othello* the play arouses horror; it attacks the nerves. The final scene in which the father in a straitjacket lies on the breast of his old nurse, murmuring the prayer with which every good Swedish child goes to sleep[4] can be rejected as a violent assault on the feelings, designed to insult, shock and reduce psychic distance; yet here Laura justifies herself with unusual metaphoric imagination: 'You were an obstacle in my path . . . I didn't plot any of this . . . it just glided forward on rails which you laid down yourself . . . if I have unintentionally hurt you, I ask your forgiveness.' He shivers and she lays her shawl on him; it drops softly against his mouth; he remembers their youthful love before crying out wildly for this cat to be taken from his chest, and for his military coat to cover him in its place.

Sailors, soldiers, huntsmen, men of primal energy, figure the demonic in their author. Ibsen kept Strindberg's portrait in his study because he liked the demonic look in his eyes, and when *The Father*, having succeeded in Denmark and in Germany, was put on in an almost empty theatre in Norway in 1891, alone in the front row sat the figure of Herr Doktor Ibsen – who had just written *Hedda Gabler*.

The captain's identity depends on faith in his child, as Othello's does on faith in his wife. He is made to destroy himself. Strindberg said in his diary that he wanted to describe 'all terrible things'. His own life, with its three stormy marriages, its lapses into madness, and critical moment of conversion, is reflected very directly in his plays so that it is all too easy to forget the skill and art that went into their composition. The states he depicts are frequent enough; but the inhabitants of mental hospitals do not produce *The Father* or *Lady Julie*. Freud himself was later to say, as he formulated by self-analysis his theory of repression, that he himself was his own most important patient.

Strindberg's three bursts of dramatic writing (1887–9, 1897–1901, 1907–9) were interspersed with periods of novel-writing, pamphleteering, and, in the mid-1890s, unusual sterility. He had been working since his early youth, always and almost compulsively writing; the plays appeared and were quickly written, often in contrasted pairs, in a matter of weeks rather than months; but they were the result of long periods of incubation. At first an avowed atheist and materialist, he passed through a period of admiration for Nietzsche, through the conversion of the 'inferno' crisis of 1897–9 to theosophy and the reading of Swedenborg. In his youth he had become an accomplished sinologist, whilst working in the Royal Library; and he now turned to Buddhism. When, therefore, he asked that on his grave should be inscribed 'Ave crux, spes unica' it was in no spirit of submission to the Lutheran establishment. The dissolution of what Lawrence was to term 'the old stable life of the ego' is the theme of the plays that were crowded into his last twenty years of life. *Lady Julie* (1889) appeared when *The Father* had already made Strindberg known in Berlin and Paris. Though banned in Sweden, its preface, the manifesto of Strindberg's new drama, introduces a play that is far richer and more complex in its lattice work of relationships, its interweaving of a season and a place. It is now frequently revived, and has provided the script for more than one fine film.

Lady Julie, victim of the struggle between her father and mother, lacks any firm central core of identity, and the meeting of her dreams with those of Jean the valet, an aggressive yet unstable compound of the socially misplaced, destroys her – in the castle kitchen among the pots and pans of Kristine, Jean's mistress, who exerts the terrible unthinking strength of the conditioned character. The delicious beauty of a Swedish midsummer night is suggested in the ballet interlude – but also the coarse country view of coupling. Without the scent of the lilacs, the sound of the fiddle and the peasants' dance, the lyric force of this play is lost. Although it could never have been embodied adequately on the stage of Antoine's Théâtre Libre, the intense beauty of the flowers that open out on half-melted snow, in the brevity of that awakening that comes so suddenly, the exhilarating taste of the air, place the action in the realm of Kore, the spring goddess. Strindberg was again to use the northern spring in *Easter*, the lakes and forests of Dalecarlia in *The Bridal Crown*, a collage of scenes in *The Great Highway*.

Every character, as Strindberg declares in the preface, is a constellation of many selves, and

> an individual who had stopped developing, or who had moulded himself to a fixed role in life, in other words, stopped growing, came to be called a character, whereas the man who goes on developing, the skilful navigator of life's river, who does not sail with a fixed sheet, but rides before the wind to luff again was stigmatized as 'characterless' because he was so difficult to catch, classify, and keep tabs on. [On the stage] a character becomes fixed in a mould . . . 'Barkis is willin' . . . Vice has a reverse side not dissimilar to virtue . . . The naturalist has abolished guilt with God but he cannot expunge the consequence of her action.

Jean, the valet, is intelligent and something of an actor. He has seen the world. He can defend himself against Julie's insults by breaking the code of master and servant, yet a few moments later can correct Kristine: 'Kindly express yourself respectfully when you refer to your mistress', to which she retorts that her own self-respect would deter his lordship's cook from 'mucking about with the groom or the pigman'. Kristine is at once entrenched in her piety and well aware that Julie 'acts strange' when 'she's got her monthlies coming on', while she cooks something to bring on an abortion for Julie's bitch who had managed to slip out with the gamekeeper's pug 'and that, Lady Julie won't allow'. Class distinction also rules the animal kingdom.

Julie, a woman of twenty-five, brutally malformed by the theories of her emancipated mother and her crazy father (as she confesses in part II) has been made to muck out the stables, yet is expected to behave with decorum. She has treated her wooer like a dog, turned to her greenfinch and her pet bitch, but she half woos the valet, whose secret childhood dreams had centred on the young lady from the castle. After the seduction he describes to her his escape through the dry-closet of the little Turkish pavillion which looked so charming. The flavour of the dialogue, crisp, direct, is set by Jean and Kristine; if Julie tries to get the better of them, they either adopt a respectful accent, which puts her at a great distance, or deflate her grandeur with some earthy wisdom. At the end of the first act Jean orders her, unsuccessfully, to retire; instead, of course, as the peasants approach singing a coarse little song, she retreats to his room.

Jean:	I'll bolt the door. And if anyone tries to break in, I'll shoot. Come (drops to his knees) Come!
Lady Julie	(urgently): You promise –
Jean:	I swear.

'Quite the little aristocrat, aren't you?' she had earlier taunted her Don Juan. But when she upbraids him with stealing her father's Burgundy he can reply that he regards himself as a child of the house, and entitled to his share. Kristine gets 'a percentage on all groceries, and a rake-off from the butcher'. When she talks piously about the blessings of confession – 'He'll take all our sins upon Him' – Jean interjects 'Including the groceries?'

The successful seduction releases in Jean a more mature daydream – running a hotel in Switzerland, on money to be procured by Julie; she will preside at the desk and sweeten the accounts with a smile while he 'salts' them. Her counter-dream of the beauties of Lake Como is deflated, and Kristine in one brutal sentence disposes of both. Jean, who had summoned up enough courage to kick the Count's boots, trembles at the sound of his bell: '"He'll ring till someone answers – and then it will be too late. The police will come – and then –"' *Two loud rings on the bell*. Shakespeare may have thought first of that little bell as prelude to death; Strindberg uses it to reinforce the main socio-psychological thrust. Julie, humiliated, desperate, under Jean's mesmeric order – given at her own request – walks out to the barn with the valet's cut-throat razor in her hand, to inflict on herself that same death he had given her pet goldfinch on-stage. This is an early sunrise that repeats the effect Ibsen achieved at the end of *Ghosts*.

Strindberg's mother had been a servant girl whom his father seduced, and afterwards married, so the psychological links with his own story are cross-sexual. Strindberg knew already the penetrative vision of one who had been broken, whose view was not bound by special codes. It could be distorted, of course, by personal refractions and by the heightened sensibility which seems to have left him exposed, like a too sensitive skin exposed to sunburn, to the fiery impact of his own impressions. Some object – a heart-shaped pebble from the Luxembourg Gardens for example – would obtrude on him with the frightening persistence of the Count's boots or his bell upon Jean. Encroaching objects are found in later plays – *Easter, The Dream Play, The Ghost Sonata*. The world becomes pervaded by the beauty of a star or a flower, the horror of the servant pasting up the windows for winter, the smell of cabbage that lingers indoors. A world that refuses to change is as horrifying as a fixed character; the changing and evanescent 'selves' of the plays are constellated in movements of love and hate, but are, when worked upon, liable to turn into their opposites. Julie ends 'the last' who shall be 'first'; the servants' life-style allows flexibility, whereas *noblesse oblige* sends her out on her fixed course.

Ability to grow, to break out of a fixed mould was, of course, at the basis of the feminist movement. Women did not want to be writers only, even professionals only. The middle classes who led the revolt were helped by those urban groupings on which the theatre depends for its life. Strindberg's wife, Baroness Wangel, née Siri von Essen, had left her first husband, an officer in the Guards, partly in order to pursue her career as an actress. Strindberg resented even while he indulged this desire of hers; he wrote parts for her, and then agonised over the chance that she was having an affair with her leading man. This marriage, which lasted off and on for seventeen years, forms the basis of so many different kinds of play that it illustrates what Eliot discovered:

> Those to whom nothing has ever happened
> Cannot understand the unimportance of events.

A short and very successful play for two women was adapted for Siri to play either role. *The Stronger*, set in a café for women, shows the triumph of Mme X, an actress, over Mlle Y, her husband's mistress. Mme X has had to adopt the tastes of Mlle Y – embroidering her husband's slippers with the tulips that Mlle Y affects; but as the more flexible, she is the stronger. Though her son was named after Mlle Y's father, she has borne him; her role in life has not been a dream.

> I suppose you hoped I'd run away? But you're the one who's run away – and now you're sitting here regretting it ever happened. But I don't regret it. One mustn't be petty. And after all, why should I want to own something that no one else wants?

The enigmatic and totally silent Mlle Y (a part which Siri could play abroad) is finally taunted as being really empty, only built to reflect the man's dreams.

* * *

A decade later, after he had passed through the crisis of madness that eventually was recorded in the *Inferno* story, and in the trilogy, *To Damascus*, Strindberg produced in the last three weeks of October 1900 twin plays, a vision of Heaven and Hell, *Easter* and *The Dance of Death*. The one achieves stillness, repose, whilst the other is the most turbulent of all his dramas, where, in this study of the love-hate relationship in marriage, the wife finally spits in the face of her paralysed husband (another soldier) then remembering his youth. But a younger generation takes a bigger part here than in *The Father*. The leading roles were related to Strindberg's sister and brother-in-law but superimposed in memory upon his own story, though there are elements of himself also in Kurt, the kinsman of the unhappy couple in *The Dance of Death*. The setting is a grim island fortress, communication is by means of a sinister telegraph, and the whole anticipates some of the effects of *Huit Clos*. This play has tended to outstrip *The Father* in revivals on the modern stage.

Easter seems to anticipate the final plays; the central figure here is a young girl, who appears as victim and redeemer. Woman as destroyer has been eclipsed in the figure ·of Eleanora, later to be played by his young third wife, the Norwegian Harriet Bosse, thirty years younger than himself. Strindberg took as his model his youngest sister Elizabeth, who had been confined for two years in a mental hospital; he believed this fragile creature bore in her own person the sins of their family; she was their sacrificial atoner. She was telepathic, and shared his intense organic sensibility. Eleanora can feel for the flowers standing out all night in the cold. The season of revival is given very precisely in the opening words:

> The double windows out! the floor scrubbed; clean curtains – yes, it's spring again! and they've hacked up the ice from the street and the willow is flowering down by the river. Yes, it's spring. And I can hang up my winter coat.

Shame, guilt and remorse for a crime committed by the head of the family (now in prison) cannot be shed so easily. A miraculous transformation by ordeal proves, however, that the prisoner is also a good man, so that one pressing creditor suddenly turns into a generous friend, since he had been succoured in early days; the new charge of theft over Eleanora miraculously rolls away. The fairy-tale of forgiveness – benevolent transformation of the ogre in a children's story, the Giant of Skinflint Mountain – reconciles the young student to his inheritance, dissolves the black winter climate (although the penalties laid upon the father are not cancelled).[5]

Strindberg's heavenly vision is once more closely linked to the new mood of the theatre, with Maeterlinck's 'drama of silence', with changes of lighting in a dream sequence; this is called up where the giant shadow of the ogre moves across the window and then dwindles. There is no action in any outer sense, but the second half of the play repeats and reverses the first half in the manner of Japanese Noh, and the style anticipates that of the 'little theatre' which seven years later Strindberg acquired for his last plays.

In the same year Strindberg wrote his Dalecarlian fantasy, the savage and tender *Bridal Crown*, which uses the story, so familiar on the stage, of the wronged country girl. She gives her illegitimate baby to the evil Fox-Midwife, but her gentleness and patience when she is condemned expiate her act, and reconcile the warring families of herself and her lover. The spiteful sister-in-law, the ghost of the child, the water sprite and the sunken church that rises from the lake, the talking fish, the stove that moves round, show a world in metamorphosis. Strindberg wrote the music for the Nekken who sits harping, 'I hope, I hope that my Redeemer liveth.' The natural world affirms its limitations, but the supernatural gleams through; poignancy lies in a blending of the earthy and the etherial, purifying but deepening the pain.

'The idea of chamber music transferred to the drama' was taken for his intimate theatre by Strindberg from Max Rheinhardt's *Kammerspielhaus*; and it was here, eight years after its first production, that *A Ghost Sonata* enjoyed its first success. This play was also written with two other plays in just over two months; its dark twin is *The Pelican*, where the unscrupulous self-centred woman appears for the last time. Written in February–March 1908, *The Ghost Sonata* continues the technique of transposing fairy-tale material into a modern urban setting. This had also been the method of *A Dream Play* (1901). As Strindberg defined it:

> Everything can happen; everything is possible and probable. Time and place do not exist; on an insignificant basis of reality the imagination spins, weaving new patterns; a mixture of memories, experiences, free fancies, incongruities and improvisations. The characters split, double, multiply, evaporate, condense, disperse, assemble. But one consciousness rules them all, that of the dreamer . . . he neither acquits nor condemns, but merely relates.

The student, once again the hero, is here a Sunday's child, possessing second sight. In the opening scene he sees a little milkmaid who later turns out to be the ghost of a girl murdered by the old man who appears as a spider at the centre of a web of power. A fantastic chain of relationships links the inhabitants of the elegant set of apartments whose façade faces the street (and into which the later scenes penetrate). Ghosts, a Mummy kept in a cupboard, a vampire cook, preside over transformations turning the beautiful hyacinth-room into a death-chamber. If sometimes the play reminds one of *Alice in Wonderland*, the student's final speech dissolves the dream like Alice's cry 'You're nothing but a pack of cards!'

First the cackling Mummy, the remains of a beautiful woman whose statue dominates the room, dissolves the ghostly assembly.

> I prefer silence. Then one can hear thoughts and read the past. Silence hides nothing. Words conceal . . . Nature has endowed man with a sense of shame which seeks to hide that which should be hid. Nevertheless the time sometimes comes when that which is most secret must be revealed, when the mask is stripped from the deceiver's face.

There could hardly be a clearer account of the uncovering of repression.

The Mummy's daughter, loved from afar by the student, has given the hyacinths pure water which they turn into colour and perfume, whilst the vampire cook has starved all with water coloured from the dreadful bottle of Japanese soy. The daughter's end is hidden by a Japanese death-screen, which is placed round the beds of the dying. The student sees the whole world as corrupt:

> There are poisons which blind and poisons which open the eyes. I must have been born with the second kind in my veins, because I can't see beauty in ugliness or call evil good – I can't! Jesus Christ descended into hell when he wandered through this madhouse, this brothel, this morgue, which we call earth.

Yet in her death, the student restores beauty to the daughter:

> Sleep dreamlessly, and when you wake again, may you be greeted by a sun that will not burn, in a home without dust, by friends without dishonour, by a love that knows no imperfections.

The dead girl's golden harp begins to whisper, light begins to fill the room, the room then dissolves and Bocklin's 'Island of the Dead' appears projected. The vision, though reinforced by music and painting, is beyond the scene itself. The dream revealed belongs to another plane of being.

Strindberg's last play, *The Great Highway*, is set in seven stations of a journey. When the protagonist, the Hunter, descends from the heights –

> for stone is stone and snow is snow
> but human nature is another thing –

he meets facets of himself in all the other figures of the fantastic scenes. At Vanity Fair he encounters a Japanese, 'a human being at last'; but this man wants to die. When asked his name he says, 'I have travelled, sinned and suffered by the name of Hiroshima, my native town!' – the last, most startling association of Japan and death.

In his final speech, the Hunter – Ishmael as he calls himself – appeals to God:

> Bless me, your creature,
> Who suffers, suffers, from your gift of life.

The strange intensity and power of this play does not really belong to the theatre; the speaker has rejected the temptation to become again an architect in 'the town of Tophet, where I built the theatre'. Yet it was in the theatre that Strindberg's restless imagination found its chosen form; and he had indeed laboured hard throughout his life at the technicalities of his craft. The role of the woman, as he also knew, derived from elements in himself. Hope is a girl-child, the 'last memory of light' the Hunter encounters before entering the Dark Wood.

* * *

The foundations of modern Russian theatre were laid across the Baltic at the turn of the century, when Chekov, already stricken by his last illness, wrote his three final plays for the Moscow Arts Theatre, where his wife was an actress. Woman here, too, appears as the victim of endurance, the figure of a future hope. The great speech of Sonia at the end of *Uncle Vanya*, of the three sisters at the end of their play, the daughters, Varya and Anya in *The Cherry Orchard*, patience and joy, all fix their eyes on some indefinite time in the future when all shall be well and all manner of things shall be well. Some have hope, some faith, some the natural ebullience of youth.

Sobornost, the religious sense of community which lay behind the practice of public confession, can reveal the ultimate nightmare – the encroaching Great Boyg, the giant, invisible troll of tedium and sloth which engulfed Ivanov, and those who hope to get to Moscow, or wherever it is that active life pulses. The vast distances of Russia (Chekov himself came from Taganrog on the Black Sea) leave only a soundless cry to the castaways, or the echo of the harp string that sounds at the end of Acts II and IV of *The Cherry Orchard*. This is repeated at the end of Strindberg's *Ghost Sonata*; and at the end of *The Master Builder* Hilde had heard harps in the air. But more completely than Ibsen or Strindberg, Chekov's is a theatre of silence, of the gaps between words, the gaps in communication between the members of a community each wrapped in his own dream, speaking his own monologue in public – perhaps humming a tune, or playing a guitar. Yet the cohesion remains strong; the puny individual cannot strike out for himself.

In *Three Sisters*, the small-town play, salvation lies in work: everyone except Andrei has some role, defined for him by a uniform. The men are army officers, Olga and Kuligin wear the uniform of high school teachers, Masha perpetual mourning, and Irina white: she too will become a teacher. Beside Andrei, his wife Natasha, the most evil character in the whole of Chekov's plays, the self-assertive female bully who drives the sisters out of their home to make room for her own children, has no such defined role; she combines the brutality of Ostrovski's matriarchs with the destructive indirectness of Strindberg's Laura. In the country, stagnation is even greater; and the humble Waffles or Firs, the wholly inarticulate, rank lower than the women, yet are ennobled as they are.

The icon of woman as victim and redeemer was to reappear in the drama of political radicals, who in the next decade developed expressionism in Germany. The sacred maternal figures, who in the period 1916–25 add humanity to the dramas of Ernst Toller, were devised in prison. Strindberg's plays dominated the German repertory in 1917 when Kaiser's *From Morn till Midnight* based the Marxist struggle on the stations of *The Great Highway*; Strindberg's blasphemies may have encouraged such parodies as Becher's *Hymn to Rosa Luxembourg*, which turns her into the crucified divinity:

> Take the flayed body
> Down from the cross . . .
> You, peerless one! you, holy one! O, woman!

These mother goddesses – faintly copied by Sean O'Casey; transformed a generation later by the youngest expressionist, Bertold Brecht – depended on complex ensemble playing, but in works of international journalism they depended also on the particular conditions of the revolutionary years, and have not gained theatrical currency beyond their own time.

The one playwright who advanced the tradition came, on the contrary, from the country with the longest theatrical tradition in Europe; he was himself highly conservative in political views, and indeed in his social attitudes generally. Pirandello, who in 1921 produced in the space of five weeks his two best plays, *Six Characters in Search of an Author* and *Henry IV*, was a respected novelist and short-story writer, who had also for a decade turned to drama. Twenty-three plays and sixteen years later, he died, the friend of Mussolini – though refusing the rites either of Holy Church or of the Fascist Party. He termed himself a futurist.

He was the heir to that comedy of masks descending from the Roman mime; a theatre where so strong were the conventions that actors could improvise, and where, therefore, the crisis of identity expressed itself naturally in terms of the mask and the face.

A play with this name by Chiarelli had celebrated the paradoxically happy cuckold who rejects his orthodox responses, and elopes with his own wife. Pirandello's first play, *Liolà*, is set in his native Sicily, where it is more important for the old peasant to have an heir than actually to beget him; when his young wife presents him with a son by Liolà, he is delighted. This theme was treated by Pirandello more than once.

His own marriage had been arranged in traditional style with the daughter of his father's business partner, a woman he was never alone with until they were married. His great drama came when, after twenty years, he was released from union with this psychotic partner whose wild hallucinations of jealousy he had patiently endured, submitting to her fantasies, trying to play things her way. The obverse of Strindberg in his respect for the marriage tie, Pirandello's private torment, his private play of masks, was projected in terms of the theatre versus everyday life in plots which at one time it was the fashion to look upon as too cerebral, too concerned with ontological dilemmas. For Pirandello himself it was all too painfully familiar. The theatre was his landscape, was what Sweden was to Strindberg, Russia to Chekov.

That's It! If You Think So (1917) centres on the identity of a veiled lady. Is she the daughter of Signora Froli, first wife of the mad Signor Ponza who thinks her dead? Or is she the second wife of Signor Ponza, whom the mad Signora Froli mistakes for her own dead daughter? Who is being collusive? The avid town-gossips in their search for facts become a set of prying destroyers, till the veiled lady finally tells them she is both: 'I am the daughter of Signora Froli . . . and the second wife of Signor Ponza . . . for myself I am nobody. No! I am whom you believe me to be.' This theme, so poignantly reminiscent of Pirandello's own role towards his wife, is inverted in the masterpiece *Six Characters in Search of an Author* (1921) which Bernard Shaw termed the most brilliant play ever written. It would be difficult by a plot-summary to distinguish between his best and his worst productions: the theatrical impact distinguishes this from those later works where, as a tired man, Pirandello worked round and round old themes. In his greatest plays there is one Eternal Now, one supreme moment round which all revolves; so, in his working life, ten years' dramatic preparation led up to the moment in 1921 when Pirandello solved the riddle of the ghosts who had haunted him.

These ghosts of the damned, whom in his preface Pirandello compares with Dante's Francesca da Rimini eternally fixed in the moment which betrayed her, come from a world more totally dislocated than Strindberg's, but not, like his or Dante's, a world of Heaven and Hell. The damnation is nearer to that of the theatre of the absurd; though closely linked with the traditions of the Italian stage, it will stand comparison with the psychiatry of much later times – for instance with John Bowlby on attachment and loss.

Psychodrama totally fails to be adjusted to the external world; the six characters (and a seventh whom they collectively create) are led by four adults, three of whom obsessively insist on playing *their* story, erupting out of nowhere into a theatrical rehearsal where one of Pirandello's plays about a ruthless cuckold is being given a run-through. The story they insist upon is, in itself, a crude melodrama of the kind that Sarah Bernhardt might have chosen as a vehicle. The characters live perpetually in that traumatic moment when the mother discovers her daughter naked in a brothel, in the arms of her

step-father, the mother's first husband. These three are wearing for
all time their tragic masks. It is almost a definition of psychological
fixation – of the prisoner or the soldier trapped in a moment of
supreme fear, perpetually enacting it in waking dreams, or night-
mares. The characters are eternally fixed, but they demand life from
the actors: 'Being alive, we desire to live in you.'

The father, leader of the troupe, realising a love affair between his
wife and his poor servant, had magisterially sent them away
together. He took his own son from her failing breast and sent him
into the country to a nurse. He had watched over the girl who was
born, the two younger children who followed. As he is Remorse, the
mother is Grief, protesting that she bore her second family only at his
orders. The poor servant, one of the humble of the earth, is newly
dead; but the step-daughter believes her mother loved him, and is
only protesting otherwise to try to convince the eldest son that she
had not abandoned him. The son (Contempt) eternally rejects those
who bore and begot him, but from whom he was sent away at birth,
never allowed to form a relationship. He, the deprived child, when
the father takes the bereaved family back to live with him, by his
hatred for the two younger children, precipitates the death of both
(murder and suicide) and the flight of the step-daughter. All the
family are distorted by 'the world of things within'. As the father tells
the theatre manager:

> Each of us has within him a whole world of things; his own world of
> things . . . we think we understand each other but we never really do . . .
> this woman takes all my pity for her as a special form of cruelty.

One of the later additions expands this: 'Each one of us has his
own reality to be respected before God, even when it is harmful to
one's very self.' But the father cries of the almost mute mother in her
mourning weeds:

> It's horrible, gentlemen, it's horrible! . . . her deafness, her mental deaf-
> ness – feelings, yes, for her children – but she's deaf, deaf to mental
> contacts, deaf, gentlemen, it's completely hopeless!

The step-daughter in the psychologically incompatible roles of being
at once her mother's bastard and her step-father's whore, feels the
moment of betrayal so deeply that as they approach it Mme Pace, the
madame of the dress shop and brothel where the girl has been trapped,
materialises: the three have conjured her into being. The father tries
to take off the step-daughter's hat – she takes it off herself, but
refuses mutely the pretty substitute he picks for her from the stock,
indicating her mourning dress, yet, on his apology, telling him coldly
not to think about it. At this point the action is broken off, but later

the step-daughter tells the climax, 'the best'. Instead of asking why she is wearing mourning, the father had said: 'Good, then! let's take it off, take it off quickly, that little dress!' So (she adds) 'with my two months' mourning in my heart, I went there behind that screen, and took off my corsets and my vest'. The mother enters to find them together. The manager protests that they can't act a scene of nudity, but she demands 'my part, my part!' The mother intervenes, explaining her own torment: 'It's all happening now. It happens all the time. My torment isn't a pretended one.' She adds that, like Mme Pace, the two small children do not exist in themselves, they are part of her torment, that is why they cling to her (they remain mute). As the moment of shame and exposure is enacted 'Fine, fine!' cries the theatre manager. 'Damned good – and then of course – curtain!' And the curtain really comes down.

The father defends their reality which is fixed for ever whilst 'your reality is a mere fleeting and transitory illusion, taking this form today and that tomorrow' and here, later, Pirandello was to philosophise at length in the additions he made about the agony of being real but not embodied.[6] When finally the baby is discovered drowned in the garden and a shot is heard from where the young boy is hiding behind a tree, the actors break in:

Some actors: He's dead, he's dead! poor little boy. O, how awful.
Others: No, no, it's only playing, he's playing dead!
The father: Playing? reality, sir, reality!

The theatre manager, like Claudius, cries 'Lights, lights!', the houselights go up, and at his 'Blackout!' he is left groping, crying 'O God, leave me a glimmer to see my way out!' A faint light shows four ghostly figures, and then the step-daughter runs shrieking with mad laughter into the auditorium and out into the foyer where her laughter echoes.

All the elements for the drama, by a spontaneous illumination of the fancy, fused together, responded and worked as a whole; it seemed to Pirandello miraculous.

> Nothing is given and preconceived. The appearance of Madame Pace is the chief example of this. Everything is in the making, is in motion. Yet for the characters the story is fixed – or rather the situation – yet because the author has rejected it, it comes out disorganized, unformed, chaotic, sidetracked.

The events have indeed to be pieced together by the audience, as an analyst has to piece together a story from conversation and dream; however, beyond all this, the author stands creating the whole, and Pirandello insists that he is not to be identified with any of the characters. It is the mother and the daughter who are fixated, it is the father who explains. The fluidity of dream belongs to the drama; the fixation of nightmare to the 'play within the play'.

Henry IV, which is closer than any other play to a dramatic monologue and has some obvious affinities with *Hamlet*, is the story of a man frozen into the eternal Now of his masquerade. When he sees the daughter of the woman he had loved twenty years before, he cries: 'Terrible wonder! the dream alive in you! more than ever it was! it was imagination; you have made it alive in person!' In Pirandello, as in Strindberg, woman is the custodian of man's dream. With the dream, drama was liberated from subservience to the literal, the prosaic; the numinous, the holy, restored transfiguration; the power returning showed the function of art. 'In dreams begin responsibilities'.[7] To experienced craftsmen, in mid-career, these dreams came suddenly, as a gift; were composed in a few weeks (one in three days); represented a peak of achievement, with much inferior material before and after. Pallas Athena sprang fully-armed from the head of Jove. In one of his more curious flights of fancy, Strindberg, detecting the influence of his own works on the latest plays of Ibsen, exclaimed 'He is my uterus and bears my seed!'

The man's work on woman's life – indeed, a great deal of social literature – had been implanted by women, written for court societies in which women played a leading role, interpreted and addressed to women. The great ladies of the Renaissance ordered their praises from their poets as the great ladies of Paris ordered their dresses from the leading houses at the time when drama also was centred in that city.

It might be maintained that in these works women in fact played the masculine role of fertilising the man's imagination; not only did Pallas spring from the head of Jove, but *all* the Muses were feminine. Envy of the feminine role as child-bearer may express itself in the most curious forms; the philosopher G. E. Moore once (linguistically, of course) spent an hour on the proposition 'No man can be a mother.' It made an interesting variation on 'No quadratic equations go to race meetings.'

Notes

1 See above, *Paris in the Bernhardt Era*, pp. 77, 79.
2 *Uncle Vanya* (1899), *Three Sisters* (1901), *The Cherry Orchard* (1904).
3 Strindberg defended the characters of Helmer in *A Doll's House* and Alving in *Ghosts*; it would not be out of character if he felt there was a case for Hjalmer Ekdal whose wife tells him ironically she does not know the paternity of Hedwig: 'How should I?'

4 I am endebted for this and several points to Professor Inga Stina Ewbank.
5 In the accusation of theft, the ogre who dwindles, and the very name Eleanora, there is a submerged reflection of *A Doll's House*, set on Christmas Eve. The indirect influence of Ibsen on Strindberg merits full examination.
6 Jennifer Lorch has written on Piteoff's production in 1923 in Paris, and its relation to the 1925 version. (The British Pirandello Society, Yearbook 1982.)
7 This is the epigraph to Yeats's *Responsibilities* (1914). Expressionism projected the mental and spiritual responses behind the 'facts'; futurism concentrated on the surface to reveal the depths, which expressionism distorted.

My Cambridge

VII.

'My Cambridge'

I completed my half century at Cambridge in 1977. In October 1927, the youngest bar one of sixty-eight young women, I came up to Girton from my northern high school to read English. To compare then and now is perhaps the simplest way to define my Cambridge.

Then, as now, to become a member of this little society was to become a citizen of the world. The sixty-eight included Monica Hunter from the Cape, Eileen Traill from the Argentine, Munira Sadek from Egypt. As Professor Monica Wilson, the first is known today throughout Africa as a brave defender of the liberties of all Africans; the second has achieved vicarious fame as the mother of Judy Innes; the third pioneered scientific education for women in her native country.

Today, with Cambridge in a 'steady state' at about twice its pre-war size, the first year at Girton averages 150 undergraduates; from a date as soon as is found practicable after 1978, these will include men. Men can be elected to the Fellowship from 1976.

Fifty years ago, although still without full membership of the university, the Fellows of the two women's colleges had been newly admitted to university posts as teachers and examiners. Girton was still issuing the certificates which it had given its younger members since 1869; so in 1930 I received one stating that I had done all that would have entitled me, if a man, to graduate as a BA. The university also supplied a degree certificate in which the word 'titular' had been inserted by hand; this came through the post. No procession to the Senate House, no family parties in the Yard. Today, undergraduates kneel to receive their degree from the first woman Vice-Chancellor, Rosemary Murray, President of New Hall.

As freshers, none of these distinctions concerned us at all; we rapidly formed ourselves into little groups known as 'college families'. Every member of the college belonged to a 'family', sat together at meals, met together at night for a collation known as 'jug', and if necessary signed one another 'out of hall'. Every morning and evening we signed the 'marking rolls' to show we were 'keeping nights' as the university required of men (though not of us).

In due course I was invited to meet one of the original five students who in 1869 joined the first College for Women, then at Benslow House, Hitchin; in 1873 it moved to within two miles of Cambridge and was renamed Girton College. Emily Gibson, Mrs Townshend, an exquisitely pretty old white-haired lady of eighty, observed, 'I will give you a piece of useful advice, my dears. If ever you have to go to prison take a change of underclothes, so they will know you are a lady; and say you are a vegetarian – the food is better if you do.' In the cause of women's suffrage, she had spent a fortnight in Holloway jail.

Set in its fifty-two acres of grounds, the college was exceptionally self-sufficient, and had a strong identity. Older members felt themselves primarily members of Girton. The founder had felt it essential to site the buildings at a safe distance, in order to retain the support of ladies who otherwise 'would have been almost ashamed to speak of it'. True, Cambridge was a riotous town, and the Vice-Chancellor had a private prison for prostitutes, which survived to the 1890s. But the choice of site has proved a handicap in modern times. It was the one fact mentioned by the BBC in announcing the decision to admit men. It is the one fact everyone knows.

For us, a college bus ran in and out, as it still does; college closed at 11.15. As always, climbing in was easy, but it could lead to questions. Rosamond Lehmann had just published her novel *Dusty Answer*, where Girton's restrictions were rather overdrawn in the interests of her beautiful and intensely sensitive heroine. Friendship at Grantchester and betrayal at The Whim put her Judith into the Cambridge of Virginia Woolf, whose style is echoed in the richly evocative set pieces of landscape painting, breathing an odour of nostalgia.

It was the first of the 'older' images of Girton I was to meet; I did not then realise that the story was essentially that of L. T. Meade's novel of the 1890s, *A Sweet Girl Graduate*. But in my second year Mrs Woolf herself came to visit Girton and Newnham, and spoke to the Odtaa Society (so called from the initial letters of 'one damned thing after another'). 'I hope your society is a great improvement on my sketch,' she wrote to the secretary; the result was *A Room of One's Own*.

Mrs Woolf contrasted the dreary meal at a women's college with a splendid lunch at King's. But I was told the meal would have been better if she had not sat so long looking at the sunset on the Backs that she came in long past the dinner hour. On the other hand, even the most opulent college does not serve *crême brulée* every day. We enjoyed Mrs Woolf but felt her Cambridge was not ours.

The university was at a peak of intellectual activity. Keynes in economics, the Cambridge school of anthropology led by Frazer and Jane Harrison, the school of archaeology in classics, the work of Moore and Wittgenstein in philosophy, the new English school led by Ivor Richards and 'Manny' Forbes kept level with the great scientists, J. J. Thomson and Rutherford.

I had come up well prepared in Shakespeare, Donne and the Romantics, but not at all prepared for the intellectual explosion of Modernist poetry and the work of Joyce, D. H. Lawrence, Virginia Woolf. The imaginative grasp of this new work came in the live exposition of our teachers, by direct contact, by hearing the words 'spoken with power', to borrow a phrase from anthropology. I was told that even the great Indian mathematician Ramanujan had known his subject in isolation, but that meeting with Hardy had alone enabled him to develop it.

Cambridge English had separated off from Modern Languages only in 1917, and the new Tripos began in 1926, introducing contemporary and comparative literature, with a good deal of social history, some aesthetics and philosophy. The men who taught it had begun by reading classics or history or moral science. We therefore discussed Aristotle's *Poetics*, read Dante and modern Americans; but above all, the poetry of *The Waste Land* gave us a new world. Once I heard Sir Herbert Grierson read aloud the poetry which, as a young man, he had recited to himself ecstatically as he walked Edinburgh's New Town; and for those moments, listening, I could feel that Swinburne might be a great poet. What Swinburne was to Grierson, Eliot was to us. Major contemporary literature was coming out all the time. To be able to go into a bookshop and buy a new volume entitled *Ash Wednesday* or *The Tower* challenged the revolutionary method of 'Practical Criticism' which Richards was expounding weekly. 'Bliss was it in that dawn to be alive!'

We met no consensus of opinion. Some lecturers held views very different from those of Richards, whose psychological theory of literary value became for some of his followers something to be accepted as revelation. The creative work being produced at Cambridge in that time was sceptical yet exhilarated. William Empson, with whom I have always been so proud to have been bracketed in the results of the Tripos examination, had first read mathematics; his mathematics was part of his poetry, in 'Legal Fiction', for instance, or 'To an Old Lady'. Kathleen Raine has spoken of his 'contained mental energy, as of a flame whose outline remains constant while its substance is undergoing continual metamorphosis at a temperature in which only intellectual salamanders could hope to live', and of 'that sense of vivid shock his presence always produced'. *Seven Types of Ambiguity* was written for Richards, who supervised his studies at Magdalene; bits of it came out in the magazine *Experiment*, where Jacob Bronowski was also publishing poetry, and some of Kathleen Raine's early poems appeared. She arrived in 1926 at Girton, reading botany. Malcolm Lowry and John Davenport were writing for the same magazine and also composing Footlights Revues for May Week. Michael Redgrave, at Queens', edited another magazine, *The Venture*. Alistair Cooke drew caricatures and wrote verses. I think he read modern languages. He founded the Mummers, the first mixed drama club.

Political debate centred on the Union Society rather than the clubs; one of my 'family' became a friend of the President, Kenneth Adam, the future director of BBC programmes. She was a keen Liberal and a member of the 80 Club; together we sat in the Gallery, for the union was not open to women, and followed the debates. Hugh Foot was President in my third year.

Nor could we at first join the dramatic societies (so I saw Dadie Rylands in feminine roles at the Marlowe Society). The musical world, however, freely admitted us, and two of my 'family' sang in Boris Ord's Madrigal Society, which then, as now, performed in May Week from punts outside King's. In college itself there were many small informal groups, like Odtaa. But the best gift was the right to be solitary and independent if one wished, as Dame Margaret Cole recorded in *Growing up in Revolution* (she came up to Girton in 1911):

> My first impression of College was one of freedom – freedom to work when you liked; to stop when you liked, to cut, even, lectures which turned out unhelpful and uninteresting; to be *where* you liked *when* you liked and with *whom* you liked (subject to not making too anti-social a racket); to get up and go to bed when you pleased and, if desirable, to go on reading, writing or talking till dawn.

Apart from the lectures (some of which were held very informally in college halls) teaching was still largely a college affair. 'Mays', the first year examination, was a semi-private intercollegiate game, of three groups. Although Richards crowded the largest room of the dreary old Arts School, one had to run smartly from Cat's to King's to Emma to hear Tom Henn, Dadie Rylands or F. R. Leavis. Sir Arthur Quiller-Couch still addressed his audience as 'Gentlemen' and was displeased when he found he had inadvertently awarded the Chancellor's Medal for English Verse to a woman, Elsie Phare of

Newnham. He would not accept us at his evening classes on Aristotle's *Poetics*.

However, our college teaching was varied. My don, Miss Hilda Murray, arranged for us to be taught Practical Criticism and the modern period by F. R. Leavis. He cycled up on Wednesday afternoons to the old army hut where classes were held, with unbuttoned shirt and a knapsack full of books. He read us Eliot, Richards and Empson (how many people have been taught poetry written by a contemporary undergraduate?); many horrendous examples came from *The Oxford Book of English Verse*. Besides Eliot, he stressed Walter de la Mare, Wilfrid Owen, Edmund Blunden and Edward Thomas. Other teachers were Joan and Stanley Bennett (she taught whilst bringing up a family of four, who sometimes interrupted the supervisions) and the terrifying Dr Pettoello, who taught Dante in a little room filled with copies of *La Libertà* (he was in exile from Mussolini's Italy). Brandishing a poker he would declare 'Firrst, you assassinate [this word was hissed] sommvon in Turin; zen you assassinate sommvon in Milano; and zat undermine zeir *morale*!' He was to be met also in the sixpenny gallery of the Festival Theatre, to which experimental productions of Goethe's *Faust* in both parts, Elmer Rice, Eugene O'Neill, Aeschylus, drew an audience from all over Europe. There I saw *As You Like It* staged in black and white, Rosalind as a boy scout blowing a whistle; *Julius Caesar* in modern dress (which must have delighted Pettoello) and most unforgettably, Flora Robson in *Six Characters in Search of an Author*.

In addition to directing our studies, Miss Murray conferred on her pupils the benefit of an Oxford point of view quite opposed to that of Cambridge. She was the daughter of Sir James Murray, editor of the Oxford Dictionary, and had begun her life by compiling index cards for that great work in a 'tin tabernacle' in her father's garden. He used his large family for enforced labour as he had, of course, no public grant. A Cambridge colleague was later to remark that she had 'one of the best memories in Europe'; her knowledge was daunting and her most caustic comments were pencilled upon our weekly offerings in a fair, round hand; but 'Have you any manuscript authority for that variant?' she once asked when I made a slip in translating Chaucer. As we trooped into her book-lined room with its colour scheme of blue and orange, we used to practise meek ways of saying 'yes'. But when at the end of my first year my father died and left a young family still to be educated, she was tenderness itself.

Bereavement and poverty and falling in love, all during the years of depression, made up my life in its personal aspects. The years 1930–6 gave me a taste of extremities which have ever since enabled me to put other difficulties in proportion. After my mother's death, with two brothers still completing their education, I had two years to wait before Miss Murray retired in 1936 and Girton elected me to a teaching fellowship. I was twenty-seven and had published three books. I started at £250 a year. My youngest brother won a scholarship that year. I was at Somerville College, Oxford from 1935–6, and witnessed the acid reception of Dorothy Sayers' *Gaudy Night*.

* * *

In 1945 I was given my first temporary university appointment. I had spent the war years in London with the Board of Trade, a most educative experience, had learnt Norwegian from the Norwegian Navy, and was writing a book on Ibsen. Post-war students were the most brilliant set; an era of intercontinental travel began for scholars. Six visits to North America, two to Australia and New Zealand, two to the Far East, many to Scandinavia, one to India, one to Kuwait, one to Hungary, one to Berlin enabled me to give students from these places some insight into problems of adjustment when they came to Cambridge. The scholars' is the only international society that really works.

Looking at Cambridge now, I see a much larger and more organised English School. With Frank Kermode, Christopher Ricks and a host of lively young people, it is not inbred, and in my view still leads the field. It still remains a college-based subject: each undergraduate may determine his own course (for example the subject of his 'long essay' which replaces a conventional paper), but this has to be centrally accepted. The combination of wide options and growing numbers (at present about 800 undergraduates) means a headache for the university computer at the time of planning examination timetables. Instead of one professor (who spent much of his time at Fowey as Commodore of the Yacht Club) there are now seven professors, four readers, twenty-seven lecturers and assistant lecturers, all reaching for their lawful allocations of leave and mostly spending it much farther off than Fowey. These numbers include the Department of Anglo-Saxon which, after spending forty years in unnatural union with Anthropology, has made a companionate marriage with English. But the total Faculty numbers 130, some living precariously on the fringe. To keep communications open, the forms of the Tripos examination are constantly being discussed, and formally laid down; for it is the subject of intense anxiety, and reassurance is constantly being sought. The present system of public grants links an undergraduate or graduate student's future much more directly to his examination.

The anxiety extends itself to general forms of university life. Changing patterns of relations depend on changing habits. Very few dons reside in college, and yearly the number grows less. Even inflation does not send them back. Those breakfast parties that I remember from the 1930s have disappeared. It may be the changing form of the college community (most dons are married and without the domestic help of former days) that has led the demand for mixed colleges; if the generations no longer combine in one community, an alternative is for the sexes to do so.

In the late 1950s and early 1960s the arrival of the new colleges for graduates (Darwin, Clare Hall, Wolfson) which were mixed from the beginning, had followed the institution of the third women's college, New Hall, which opened in 1954.

* * *

Cambridge seemed to run a steady course through the 1950s and early 1960s. In 1966 in California I met the Berkeley students' protest movement, and Marcuse, who was also there. He greatly impressed the impressionable with his unending flow of clichés. About two years later, Californian attitudes became fashionable in Cambridge, and reforming the university became an alternative to study.

Handicapped by the science students' preference for their labs, and by the lack of a strong social science department, Cambridge was assisted by the strong sense of guilt which such exceptional opportunities and privileges could generate (a form of egoism, of course, if the privileges are taken as being merely gratuitous and not a public investment). A few students created a few incidents, though often heavily reinforced from outside. On one such occasion, when honorary degrees were being conferred, a group began yelling 'Intellectuals in! Adrian out!' outside the Senate House Yard. They had mistaken the Chancellor, Professor Lord Adrian, for an hereditary peer, not realising that as the discoverer of the D waves in the brain, he had more intellect in his little finger than the whole bunch of them put together. He walked on with the puzzled look of one whose experiment is showing unusual features. But I hated that chant. It had exactly the rhythm of 'Sieg Heil! Sieg Heil!'

Good sense and a sense of humour were not wanting. Among the *graffiti*, the inscription 'Give me back my mind' provoked the retort underneath: 'No – you must find it for yourself'; and 'Is there intelligence left on earth?' was met by 'Yes – but I'm only visiting.'

The relation of senior and junior members has changed much more than the forms of academic study. The ritual of being chased by the Proctor and his 'bulldogs' is being succeeded by the institutionalising of 'sit-ins' for which, as I understand, a sort of code is being drawn up. The 'Rites of Spring' generally occur in the second half of the Lent Term; the university is not sufficiently settled in the

Michaelmas Term, and in the Easter Term other interests take precedence.

For the don, it has become more necessary than ever to listen to the words behind the words. The undergraduates are now of legal age; many have travelled widely; their newspapers are filled with appeals to aggression. 'Shock report slams Tutors', screams the headline – and then somewhere, in much smaller print, the report that only a tiny fraction said they were not proud to be members of their college. Publicity is sweet for the undergraduate (it may mean a cheque and ultimately a job); so the desired image is produced. On the whole, because Cambridge is found enviable, the image will either be that of the old world of privilege (blazers and boaters and champers and *crème brulée*), or it will be Sex Probe at King's. Students are news, and sex is news; both together –!

The attitude of Cambridge to women has always been ambivalent. In 1875 a Cambridge hostess wrote after a dinner party: 'My dear, she was a nice girl, with rosy cheeks and nice manners and nicely dressed, and you wouldn't have thought she knew anything!' In her talk to the freshers in 1927, the Mistress concluded, 'And remember, my dears, the eyes of the Cambridge ladies will be ever upon you!', advising us to don hat and gloves at Storey's Way. As late as 1920, an undergraduate referendum had voted by a majority of 2329 out of 3213, to exclude women from full membership. It was thirty years and more after they had gained the national franchise that women were permitted to vote in the Councils of the university; full rights came in 1948. Yet when I was at Oxford in 1936, whilst I had already examined for Cambridge University, I found there ladies much senior to myself who had never so officiated. ('I prefer justice to favours', one of them remarked haughtily.) Girton and Newnham were built only by the co-operation of Cambridge men, who taught their undergraduates, spoke for them, served on their governing bodies (at Girton till 1952). In the last eight years, during my Mistress-ship, men took over our teaching posts, if women were not available – Christopher Morris, a Fellow of King's, for some years directed studies in history; economics is now directed by another member of King's; German taught by a Fellow of Magdalene; and of the 280 supervisors on the Girton lists of teachers, the majority are inevitably men, since Cambridge is still predominantly a men's university.

At the end of *Dusty Answer* Rosamond Lehmann wrote:

> Farewell to Cambridge, to whom she was less than nothing. She had been deluded into imagining that it bore her some affection. Under its politeness, it had disliked and distrusted her and all other females, and now it ignored her.

'Of course I am entirely without prejudice', remarked a committee member once. 'I would always prefer a first-class woman to a third-class man.'

One or two of the Girton Fellows now hold joint teaching posts at other colleges (they are certainly first-class women); at Jesus College Jacob Bronowski's daughter, the first woman Fellow, has been admitted after progressing from Newnham to a Fellowship at Girton, from Girton to King's. Another Girtonian went to Clare, another to Churchill, yet another directs studies and lectures at Trinity. But this is to anticipate the story of the last decade.

I had been Mistress of Girton for about two weeks when in October 1968 a printed note through the post informed us that one of the men's undergraduate colleges was going to admit women at all levels. The motives of senior and junior members did not necessarily or even probably coincide. Pressure for co-residence (co-education already existed) came mainly from undergraduates who evinced a sometimes explicit desire to have more girls about. The Fellows were concerned to maintain standards in threatened subjects ('We thought we might get a few good classics,' one senior tutor blandly observed). In general it was favoured by the young and opposed by the older generation of dons.

What happens in the universities is closely dependent on what happens in the schools, but here again stands a big question mark. The boys' public schools are increasingly admitting girls; the girls' public schools have not, to my knowledge, reciprocated. Yet the women's colleges at Oxford and Cambridge have never been dependent on the large girls' public schools, and have always drawn from hundreds of smaller establishments up and down the country. More than 200 schools every year send in candidates for Girton. What the Ministry does to these will react upon us directly.

It was therefore decided quite soon to introduce a new statute which would offer the chance for Girton to admit men at any time it wished to do so. This enabling statute went through the elaborate procedure of being approved by the Queen in Council, thus freeing the college to decide for itself by a simple vote. The decision of a women's college to admit men is certainly not simply the converse of the men's decision to admit women. No woman can fail to rejoice that the splendours of King's and Trinity are now opening to her sex or conceal the pleasure she feels at seeing the young women look so completely and easily at home. In their search for a new image to replace Castle Adamant, women's colleges will need to develop a creative response which utilises their own previous experience and blends it with the changing needs of the present and future time.

Among the men's colleges that have admitted women, the different atmospheres have already established a very different degree of popularity in the schools. The academic issue is largely of keeping the balance of subjects to ensure a full community. If the feminine trend to arts is not reversed, we shall end with a polarised society where men read science and women arts. The government asks Cambridge for a fifty-fifty ratio. English, the most popular faculty for women, is already over-subscribed; this is true of other arts faculties, even in terms of the colleges, certainly of the university. Medicine alone has a 'quota'.

Given the present pace of change, Girton's strong feminist image is now part of history. The exasperating stamina of the obsolete image of Cambridge or the obsolete image of Girton may be contrasted with the efforts to fix or establish an identity in the instant universities of the 1960s. The 'absolute' and intransigent quality of the Girton image has been academic, not social in its origins, and sprang from a conviction that women must prove themselves by following the exact course, be it good or bad, that had been set for men. This was proved more than a hundred years ago, when three young women answered the Tripos papers in the University Arms Hotel, watched by their chaperon. The impulse to iconoclasm is strong, but should be resisted; transformation, not destruction of the image will ensure continuity. 'Girtona Unisex' is too hard to sell.

The Cambridge image is remarkably constant too; from Rosamond Lehmann's *Dusty Answer* of the 1920s, to Charlotte Haldane's *I Bring Not Peace* of the 1930s, Andrew Sinclair's *My Friend Judas* of the 1950s, to the latest manifestation, Frederic Raphael's *The Glittering Prizes*, a return to the same intense recollected image that is an image of the writer's youth, goes with a sense that the student's life is a public role to be played out.

Yet alongside the images, a stream of quiet traditional life flows, which isn't news and never seeks this kind of projection. There are as many different Cambridges as there are graduates, and for some Girtonians, a mixed college may amputate them from their own past. At a gathering of former students, an old lady looked round Woodlands Court with disfavour. 'When I was up, none of this was here!' My placatory 'When I came up, only half of it was here,' produced little softening. So, one of the older Fellows at supper – 'All these husbands!' 'Only one each,' I said. My Cambridge, always changing yet the same, like the flowing Cam, presents me with a series of images, not one clear, distanced view. Seasons return. The Fellows of Girton were kind enough to elect me to a Life Fellowship, but I told them I wished it could have been a Research Fellowship, the title I had held more than forty years before. For that represented what I felt it to be for me.

So I am still part of Cambridge, living in a little house between the one where Lord Ramsey, the former Archbishop, was born and the haunted house of the Christ's College Ghost, at the corner of Croft Holme Lane. I can still enjoy Gregorian chants in St John's College Chapel; the insight of a pupil that comes with a shock of delight and instruction to the teacher; strawberries and cream in Neville's Court; the Japanese Society of Visiting Scholars in English; the eights rowing up to Jesus Lock before breakfast through the November mists; the lecture that sends me rushing to the University Library, and then writing furiously into the small hours; the fresh young voice uttering some platitude with awe and wonder; the sight of the Vice-Chancellor bicycling through crowds of shoppers with every lineament proclaiming the need to breast Castle Hill before half-past three; the triple bob major from the tower of Great St Mary's; the old drunk cadging money in Market Square; the hideous proliferation of bogus college or university ties, scarves, tee shirts donned by the most unsuitable visitors.

Doesn't Cambridge make you feel (asked the local councillor at the sherry party) when you go to London, that you are living in an ivory tower?

VIII.

Queenie Leavis: The Dynamics of Rejection

(7 December 1906–17 March 1981)

In the Michaelmas Term of 1927, as a fresher at Girton College, I 'kept' in A8, next to the double set of Queenie Roth, third-year Major Scholar in English. If never invited into A7, I could not but observe the Spartan life of my neighbour, her bare walls and mantelpiece, the loads of books she took in, and in which she scribbled caustically, though they were from the Library (by now probably rating as *adversaria*). In 1929 her engagement present was a bicycle which F. R. Leavis taught her to ride. I found her in the gyp wing, picking thorns out of her legs, for she had ridden into a hedge. 'Isn't Frank a lovely name?' she exclaimed to me in an unprecedented burst of confidence. Her previous exercise of walking the 'Girton grind' – to improve her sense of rhythm, as she said – was sometimes taken book in hand, oblivious of autumn tints or Maytime blossom.

She bought a row of bright little coffee cups from the Artificers' Gild on King's Parade and stood them symmetrically along her mantelpiece. She also bought a scarlet satin blouse of startling brilliance. In the summer of 1929, our don, Hilda Murray, gave a 'Star Party'; Queenie had been elected to the Ottilie Hancock Fellowship, I had acquitted myself well in Part I of the Tripos. We played Miss Murray's excruciating party games, with names pinned on our backs – I cheated and was sternly rebuked by Queenie.

That summer of 1929, she married and departed to a little house named 'The Criticastery'; within a year or so the Leavises had returned to his family home – a pleasant Victorian villa with a small orchard where Leavis scythed the grass – at 6 Chesterton Hall Crescent (it is now demolished). Queenie quickly learnt to hang modern reproductions, wear neutral tweeds and bake cakes for her Friday teas, like other Cambridge ladies. Alistair Cook, a gangling young man from *Granta*, with a large cameo ring, was there when the new periodical was being discussed. '*Sc-r-r-utiny!*' crunched

Lionel Knights through his teeth, as though grinding nuts. 'I like that!' The spirit of an innocent radical militarism was abroad.

Within an accepted social circle, ritual insults become part of its training. 'They're harmful only to gentlemen. They wouldn't hurt you in the least' is a quip from Charlotte Haldane's *I Bring Not Peace* (1932), depicting the group Malcolm Lowry termed 'Chaddie Haldane's addled salon', who met at Roebuck House, Old Chesterton.

If Leavis had been called to account by the Vice-Chancellor in 1925 for his use of James Joyce's *Ulysses* (then banned in England), in that same year the *Sex viri* had required J. B. S. Haldane to resign his Readership when cited as Charlotte's co-respondent in a divorce case.[1] He promptly brought a civil action against that body, and won it. (Haldane was a card-carrying Communist.)

In fact, I. A. Richards had been lecturing on Joyce for some time; and as in 1927 Leavis gained a probationary Faculty Lectureship, he must have soon recovered. His reaction to any opposition was an act of shock and horror. 'Dickens? Dickens?' he once gasped in a question period after his lecture to some unfortunate young man, choking for breath, tearing off the tie he put on to speak in the Library at Emmanuel, behaving like someone's maiden aunt who has heard a dirty word.

Of the horrors he had actually known between 1914 and 1918 he never spoke – they were reflected in reading a handful of poems, Owen's 'Strange Meeting', the first section of *The Waste Land*, Pound's *Hugh Selwyn Mauberly*, Rosenberg, the 'Mad Prince's Song' of de la Mare, with its echo of *Hamlet*. (The only Shakespeare he used in practical criticism at Girton was Macbeth's 'Tomorrow and tomorrow and tomorrow' – a part he had played at school.) Leavis should have been able to share what could not be spoken of with Stanley Bennett, Fellow, Director of Studies in English and Librarian at Emmanuel, for Stanley had been through it all, and lost a foot on the Western Front. Rosemary Grylls informs me that her friendship with the Bennetts led to Leavis and Queenie first meeting socially at a Girton tea-party, Stanley presiding.

In his bachelor days, Leavis had been welcomed by Stanley's wife, Joan Frankau, whom he had married in 1920, to the Bennett home. There had been picnics on the river with the lively Bennett children, when Leavis dived in to retrieve Joan's watch, even shared holidays. Leavis's abrupt exit from Emmanuel – which he described as being unceremonious[2] – was the result, Girton understood, of Queenie's hostility to Joan Bennett; any attack on Joan would certainly have roused Stanley's implacable antagonism. Queenie's own trauma had been rejection by her Orthodox Jewish family when she married a gentile. At Girton there is a letter dated October 1925 from her

brother Leonard, then at Clare and President of the Cambridge
Hebrew Congregation, asking the Mistress to permit his sister, Miss
Q. D. Roth to attend Friday meetings, which did not end till 10.30,
and saying he thought other young ladies might attend also, but if the
Mistress desired, he would provide a chaperon. We were given to
believe that after her marriage, Queenie's family read the burial
service for her.

Joan Bennett, of a more liberal Jewish family, educated at
Wycombe Abbey, Hamburg and Paris, then at Girton, being only a
year younger than Leavis, was like him a probationary lecturer,[3] and
followed a similar range of subjects – Milton and the seventeenth-
century poets, the Victorian novel; but always with an open mind, a
scrupulous concern to put alternative points of view. She was a born
teacher – patient with the dullards, genuinely concerned with drawing them out; but she was one of the 'haves', and Queenie was one of
the 'have nots'.

The Leavises broke with the Bennetts and broke soon after with
the Richardses, with whom, while Richards was Queenie's super-
visor in research, they had been on close terms. Dorothea Richards
told me she thought Queenie regretted having been too open about
her Jewish feelings. She had said that if she came into a room where
there was another Jew, their eyes met and a bond was immediately
established. Queenie now began to impose absolute choices on other
friends. Gwyneth Lloyd Thomas, one of the Girton Fellows, was told
she must 'choose' between friendship with the Richardses and
friendship with the Leavises and when she replied 'I don't see the
necessity', was told, 'Then you have already chosen.' Perhaps that
was what her family had said to Queenie.

1932 saw the award of the PhD to Queenie, the publication of her
work as *Fiction and the Reading Public*, her election to the University's Amy Mary Preston Reid Scholarship (the first woman to gain it),
the foundation of *Scrutiny*, the publication of Leavis's *New Bearings
in English Poetry* and his appointment as Director of Studies at
Downing College.

Girton was the only college where both Leavises taught – he from
1925 till the late 1930s. Miss Murray always stood staunch friend to
both – in spite of an evident lack of college spirit, noted by the
Mistress, Queenie in 1928 had been awarded the Thérèse Montefiore
Memorial Prize, which almost covered a year's fees in those days.
Miss Murray was almost the only senior member of the Faculty they
never quarrelled with; she reviewed for *Scrutiny* G. K. Chesterton on
Chaucer, with all the acidulous scholarship they could require.

Bright and precocious, even more ignorant of the world than the
rest of us, in love with her teacher (Leavis was eleven years her

senior), Queenie brought to the partnership the kind of energy that Susannah Ibsen gave to the great iconoclast she married. In her latest years, Susannah confided 'When we were young, many so-called friends came to Ibsen, but I sent them away . . . Ibsen had no steel in his character – but I gave it him.'⁴ The difference was, that unlike Susannah, Queenie had claims in the same subject as Leavis.

The claim in the Retrospect to *Scrutiny* – 'We *were* that Cambridge', the true Remnant, the chosen Minority – was very necessary to both. To the first number of *Scrutiny* Queenie contributed a review of the work of Stuart Chase, which lies close to the material of Leavis's first pamphlet *Mass Civilization and Minority Culture* (Minority Press, 1930). Here he had quoted a letter sent to her for her questionnaire on the novel. Before the marriage, he had published only one or two reviews in *The Cambridge Review*. After F. L. Lucas had noticed Queenie's book unfavourably, this journal was regarded as reprobate, part of the menacing 'discipline of letters' castigated in *Scrutiny*. Gwyneth Lloyd Thomas wrote a squib on Queenie which employed her own favourite adjectives:

> 'Alert', 'pure' and 'ascetic', see her stand
> 'The guardian of integrity'; her eyes
> Quell and put down the timid wavering hand
> And still the 'Please, teacher's ere they arise . . .
> But what did Cromwell say in 1645?

(This was, 'I beseech you, in the bowels of Christ, think it possible you may be mistaken'.)

To be an insider for *Scrutiny*, it was necessary to be an outsider. Queenie's contributions, mostly in the form of reviews, displayed her fighting style at its most withering in handling Dorothy Sayers, Virginia Woolf's *Three Guineas*, the Lady Novelists and the Lower Orders or, in 'The Discipline of Letters', Oxford's Merton Professor. Leavis's style – and his young men copied him – was evasive, full of hints, of the oblique thrust and the haughty sniff: 'The corollary . . . does not need stating explicitly' or 'There is no need to enlarge upon' or 'It is not for nothing that' – all the complicities of Minority. It claimed to be 'urbane' and 'poised'. Queenie went in for straight tackling in the St Trinian's style, with such vigorous and well-aimed thumping and jumping that the enjoyment of her vitality was stronger than the thought of the victim's discomfiture. Compared to the insults devised nowadays in television interviews, the abrasiveness of the Leavises was mild, but it was not so by the standards of half a century ago. Queenie was the more masculine, Leavis the more indirect and feminine. The need for 'an armed and conscious minority' to resist 'the overthrow of minority values' had been proclaimed in *Fiction and the Reading Public*, since of existing journals 'there is scarcely one left whose liberty of speech has not been sold to the advertiser or mortgaged to vested interests' (pp. 270–2). The saving remnant was linked with the idea of an 'organic community' in *Culture and Environment* (1933), a book to which Queenie subsequently laid claim for part authorship (see Boris Ford's note, in *The Times*, 26 March 1981). It is certainly 'odd', to use a *Scrutiny* word, that Queenie's name never appeared among those of the editors of the journal, for the work that she did was subsequently acknowledged, when the journal was reprinted in 1963, by all contributors assigning their rights to Dr and Mrs Leavis, and by the handsome share accorded her in *Selections from 'Scrutiny'* (2 vols, 1968). On the other hand Harding and Knights, who both offered to resign as editors because they could not do very much, were persuaded to stay – but Knights subsequently attacked (in a letter to *The Times Literary Supplement*, 3 March 1972). Leavis retained one or two friends from early days, chief perhaps being Henri Fluchère; Queenie's confidences to Storm Jameson in November 1948 are the unique example known to me of a natural, friendly response.[5] Here she claims part-authorship also of *The Great Tradition* which had just appeared, describes the horror of being diagnosed as suffering from cancer at thirty-eight (she was actually close on forty-two) when 'one has a young family and no relatives'. Storm Jameson from the USA had sent twelve dozen eggs and these were being enjoyed by the children. Yet when Basil Willey, who had also received a food parcel, took it round, remembering the young family, he found it dumped back on his doorstep with the words 'We don't need your charity.' The Leavises often generously housed students in difficulties: but unacceptable views met with the treatment that Boris Ford has recorded.

Queenie's projected work on *The Lives of the Humble* (Francis Place and his like) never materialised, her book on Jane Austen was never completed, but her ideas and social interests gradually permeated *Scrutiny*. Leavis swung over to the novel and to social implications of literature, and after *Scrutiny* ceased to appear, in 1953, the Leavises' need of rejection led to increased onslaughts on the insider who was really an outsider. Leavis's last decade at Downing (1952 –62) was embittered by a break with his friend Cuttle, a total break with the placable Keith Guthrie, the Master, and the notorious affair of the Richmond Lecture. What he said about Snow was no stronger than the things Queenie had said about other novelists, but to deliver this as a lecture, which was 'leaked' only by accident, made the situation more embarrassing, especially as it was an honour conferred on him by Downing. The college made him an Honorary Fellow, its highest acknowledgement, an honour which he resigned after they had failed to implement for his successors the plans that an endowed lectureship should be awarded with his own retention of the power of veto. (The connection between the two events is of course not unequivocal.) At this time, as Chairman of the Faculty Board, I used to receive the customary 20-page letters of protest and denunciation. I cheated again and asked the Secretary to read them, giving them to me only if action were required. The exacerbation of the nerves was too strong. Two of my brothers had once been pupils of Leavis, he would still behave amicably at times, though he and Queenie appeared at a Faculty meeting to denounce the proposed new Tripos option on the Novel with a fury that is unforgettable (their actual arguments now escape me). At this time Queenie also began applying for fellowships and lectureships, in which she was unsuccessful, being then in her late fifties.

After Leavis's retirement she began publication on the Victorian novel – the piece on *Wuthering Heights* in *Lectures in America* (1969), several pieces in *Dickens the Novelist* (1970) an edition of Mrs Oliphant's *Miss Marjoribanks* (1969) and a reprint of her *Autobiography and Letters* (1974).[6] There was also a paperback re-issue of *Fiction and the Reading Public* (1979) and the lecture on 'The Englishness of the English Novel' printed just before her death in the spring (1981) issue of *The New Universities Quarterly*. What begins to emerge is a picture of the Victorian heroine, in a warm, sympathetic study that accords full justification to Esther Summerson in *Bleak House*; 'a sensitive child who suffers from the "wound" received in childhood' that makes her 'undertake to atone by being useful and trying to win love' Although 'Esther can hardly believe people when they tell her how useful, pretty and loveable she is, and writes it all down to be able to' (*Dickens the Novelist*, pp. 212–13). *Miss Marjoribanks*, the dry social comedy of 1865, in which the heroine manages her little community, is seen, it is true, as the precursor of *Middlemarch* (for Queenie became very fond of these genealogies), but Mrs Oliphant herself emerges also as just the model that might encourage a woman of letters. Insufficiently rewarded, sometimes too outspoken to be printed, 'she had a great deal of experience of life as a struggle and an exposure to all kinds of hardship and disenchantment'; Anne Thackeray Ritchie wrote of her, 'She was one of those people whose presence is even more than *a pleasure*, it was a stimulus; she was kindly, sympathetic, and yet answering with that chord of intelligent antagonism which is so suggestive and makes for such good talk' (*Autobiography*, pp. 10–11 of Introduction). Even A. C. Benson and J. M. Barrie are allowed to pay tribute, and other unexpected names appear in the final article, where the 'brave heretical heroines' are distinguished as 'though modest, sensitive and conservative . . . in any crisis prepared to act in defiance of the conventions, if their sense of what is just prompts them to do so' (*New Universities Quarterly*, 35 (1981) 149–71). The choice is not unexpected, except that one heroine of Arnold Bennett is presented; the peroration comes with extracts from George Eliot, as always a chief exemplar of the struggle. 'Francophil snobs' are castigated; Miss Mitford's *Our Village* is singled out, whereas *Jude the Obscure* is 'too skeletal'. The author of *Fiction and the Reading Public* believes that the novel in England can reflect social, political and religious sentiments without becoming a novel of ideas; television, cinema and radio have some connection with 'what is generally recognised to be the imminent decay and apparent death of the English novel as a major art (though not of course of English fiction as commercial entertainment)'.

Some people can live only by using a kidney machine. The newer, mellower Queenie seems to have existed only as a reader and writer. Her protest against being addressed as 'Mrs Q. D. Leavis' (*The Listener*, 21 March 1968) and her question soon afterwards 'does he not expect to be rewarded for outstanding ability and distinguished achievement by a salary, status and even a pension?' are faint echoings of such actions as her shutting the door in the face of the child from next door, Jana Kodicek, who called to bid her welcome to Bulstrode Gardens and ask if she could be of help: 'We have our friends. We don't need any more.' Behind the 13-foot fence erected round their garden the Leavises lived secluded; she in his last illness nursed her husband devotedly, but when Ivor Richards wrote, with some effort, to congratulate Leavis on receiving the CH in the 1978 New Year Honours (Richards himself having been awarded it some years before) Queenie returned a letter of such virulence that Richards threw it away. The editor of *The Cambridge Review*, a few months before her death, writing to ask of some account of her life received a lengthy missive beginning 'I am astonished at being confidently approached by a professor of the Faculty which has for fifty years boycotted and persecuted my husband and myself in spite of our incomparable services to English studies here, a faculty of which some members published defamatory obituaries of him in the newspapers at his recent death; or by the Master of a college which treated so infamously its most emenent alumnus in the Humanities', with further castigation of 'the Bennetts and their successors', i.e. the editor himself.

If Queenie's early self-effacement in favour of her husband was in the interests of a career that her zealotry had not forwarded, her final re-emergence is, as a historian of the Victorian novel, surprisingly conservative, not averse from the drudgery of footnotes, 'the dull duties of an editor', and beautifully responsive to the best portions of an uneven work of genius like *Wuthering Heights*. This late-achieved power deserves recognition of the kind she herself gave to that spirited and overworked lady, Mrs Oliphant.

Notes

1 See Ronald Clark, *J. B. S. Life and Work of J. B. S. Haldane* (Hodder & Stoughton, 1968), ch. iv.
2 See the article by John Harvey, 'F. R. Leavis: an appreciation', *Encounter*, 52, 5 (May 1979), 59–67. Then as now, the loss of a college base was even more crippling than the lapse of a temporary university junior appointment. The queue for promotion was long; in the hungry thirties many young men of promise went elsewhere.
3 Details of the university appointments in the crucial years 1927–36 were given by Noel Annan, *TLS*, 12 December 1975, p. 1488.
4 Bergliot Ibsen, *De Tre* (Oslo, Gyldendal Norsk Forlag, 1948), p. 237.
5 Storm Jameson, *Journey from the North*, 2 vols (Collins & Harvill Press, 1969–70), II, 234–5.
6 She also wrote Introductions for *Jane Eyre* and *Silas Marner* in the Penguin Classics.

IX.

'The Lyf So Short, The Craft So Long to Lerne': Poetry and Other Works of Kathleen Raine

When, at seventy-three, she published her *Collected Poems 1935 –1980*, Kathleen Raine cut out more than half the lyrics from her earlier *Collected Poems* of 1956, her first slender volumes of 1943, 1946 and 1949 being almost obliterated; these she said represented not the achievement of a young poet, but the juvenilia of an old one.

If her contemporary and friend, William Empson, had composed no verse after his early thirties, her first major achievement came in her mid-forties. Another friend, Edwin Muir, like W. B. Yeats, reached full maturity only in his sixties; yet all three had devoted themselves from youth both to the craftman's problem of language, and to philosophy; for some years Kathleen Raine lived by translating. An individual yet traditional form, a strongly wrought personal myth, rhythm and resonance that pulses through and sustains an eloquent pause, can be achieved only after years of endeavour; then it is 'given'.

Two poems of Kathleen Raine, at once her supreme triumph and the key to her work as a whole, achieve new forms; these are 'Northumbrian Sequence' from *The Year One* (1952), and the elegy *On a Deserted Shore* (1973). After publishing the first, she endured a dozen years' barrenness, when poetry forsook her as her personal story worked out to a conclusion. She published her first *Collected Poems* whilst intellectually building the principles of her own poetic.

Her second reputation as a Blake scholar of international distinction emerged from 1946 to 1962 as a Research Fellow at Girton College, Cambridge, where she had studied thirty years before; in 1962 she gave the Mellon lectures on *Blake and Tradition* at Washington DC. Two years later she returned to poetry with *The Hollow Hill* (1964); four small volumes appeared in the 1970s, whilst an international reputation both as a poet and scholar led to lectures and many articles in English and foreign journals, translations of her poetry, which is as widely appreciated in France, Spain and Italy as in England; finally her co-editorship of the periodical *Temenos*, devoted to the art of the imagination.[1]

Separated by more than twenty years, the two sequences share visionary and personal themes of the sacred places where eternal powers enter mortal life, evoking particular North Country scenes which are the necessary sources of power for Kathleen Raine; and the entry into her life of Gavin Maxwell, the man whose death is lamented in the elegy. The 'message' lies in the rhythm and cadence[2] – in both poems the rhythm of prayer. In the fourth section of the sixfold 'Northumbrian Sequence' it bursts out with sudden energy as invocation and incantation, half-command and half-plea.

> Let in the wind,
> Let in the rain,
> Let in the moors tonight.
>
> The storm beats on my windowpane
> Night stands at my bed foot,
> Let in the fear,
> Let in the pain,
> Let in the trees that toss and groan,
> Let in the North tonight.
> Let in the nameless, formless power
> That beats upon my door

The section ends

> Let in the wound,
> Let in the pain,
> Let in your child tonight.

Echoes reverberate of the *Lyke Wake Dirge*, of *Wuthering Heights* and of Blake's 'virgin fears' that tremble before the invading power of an Annunciation, such as that terrifying Annunciation celebrated by Yeats.[3] Sections 5 and 6 embody two visionary moments of perfection described in Kathleen Raine's autobiography. A waking vision of a young boy sleeping under a Rowan tree in which a bird sang; this came to her as a benediction on the re-entry into the lost Paradise of her childhood which she found at her first meeting with Gavin Maxwell. The second was an experience of being out of her body, which as a child in Northumberland she experienced in sickness.[4] But these two sections do not carry the same imprint of new powerful rhythm which in the previous section is imposed by the alternation of very short lines and occasional long ones. The gaps or pauses, inhalation and exhalation, marked by reiteration of very brief keywords, had been used for an effect of terror and possession in a poem entitled 'Invocation' that appeared in her first volume, *Stone and Flower*. It ends

> if only the lips may speak
> if only the god will come.

but the ritual is violent without being forceful.

In 'Northumbrian Sequence', where the god has come in storm, the movement becomes authoritative, ceremonious, very heavy, as in Emily Brontë's 'Last Lines'

> O God within my breast,
> Almighty, ever present Deity!

Twenty years were to pass before this invasion by the Animus (in Jungian terms) was complemented by the serene, meditative rhythms of the second sequence. In 1973, *On a Deserted Shore*, a sequence of 130 short poems, embodied the new form which Kathleen Raine has increasingly refined, and which is her most original discovery. The individual florets of this composite form in some ways resemble the Japanese haiku, as she has herself observed; the haiku, however, is a strict three-line verse of seventeen syllables, arranged 5-7-5, whereas her verses may run to six or seven lines. The pause or turn within the stanza – for each while complete in itself is also a stanza of the whole – modulates the perspective, and is the signature of a break in feeling. It is part of the mourning ritual. Alternation of long and short lines is notable in many elegies – the final choruses of *Samson Agonistes*, in *Adonais*, and *In Memoriam*; it may represent the physical act of bowing, the control of breathing, in prayer.

On the shore of the Hebridean Paradise recalled in these poems she recited the final lines of *Samson Agonistes*, and a mantra given her by an Indian friend (see *The Lion's Mouth*, pp. 149, 75). She has described a dream of her fellow poet, Edwin Muir, which was 'a very simple one; it consisted of a semi-colon' (*Defending Ancient Springs*, p. 2). This meant that the poet never knows all he writes – beyond the semi-colon is something that completes his meaning. 'We can never define it, yet it is also part of the poem, and part of what the poet communicates to the reader.'

Whilst the wintry 'Northumbrian Sequence' marked the beginning of her relationship with Gavin Maxwell, the Spring and Summer beauty of the Scottish west coast and islands transforms the mourning for his death; and with it, the deeper mourning that came when he denied that they had ever shared a vision of the lost Paradise of childhood.

> Time was
> When each to other was a glass,

And I in you and you in me beheld
Lost Paradise,
With every tree and bird so clear
Regained it seemed:
We did not guess how far
From the heart's mirror the reflected star.(51)

Memory; beyond recall
The linnet's song,
The clover scented air:
Yet we were there,
My love and I together in one house.
Home is the sum of all
The days that sheltered us:
The place of no return.(6)

A night in a bad inn –
But I would say
Guest in love's house;
And blessed and thrice blest
Who walk on earth's sweet grass,
Bathe in time's stream
And under green boughs rest –
Too short a stay.(44)

If this were illusion, elsewhere she says, yet 'that dream is all I am.'

Into the gaps, rhythmically and syntactically created, the reader inserts his own response. The frequent elision of the verb to be, as in 51 and 44, produces a sense of timelessness, of an eternal now, while the mood (in the sense that one speaks of moods of a verb) is that of prayer. Prayer never gets beyond the semi-colon, it is always partly unformulated.

The inclusion of material beyond the explicit is found in drama through visual symbols of movement, gesture or grouping, the 'dumb poesy' of Lear's kneeling to Cordelia, or Hermione's statue in movement; both indicate resurrection, or the return of the dead. On funeral monuments the broken column or the concealing draperies invite completion by the imagination.

The haiku is constructed to be presentational in the same way:[5] intensely concentrated upon the senses, it offers the reader an imaginative launching into his own version, partly self-created:

Summer grasses –
All that remains
Of soldiers' visions.

(Written by Matsuo Basho at the Castle on the Height, where an army died.)

> The world of dew is
> A world of dew . . . and yet
> And yet . . .

Of her own elegaic form, Kathleen Raine has said:

> They [the stanzas] look easy, but they're not. They're a very structured
> form in reality, very small structured forms like diatoms or minute
> organic forms. But again, in the last few years, I have felt a compulsion to
> write in this particular form. They are, as it were, given me. (*LL*, p. 55)

It allows great variation in the relation of the parts to the whole (like
Chaucer's daisy flower, Compositae, made of many florets). Of
course it is not totally without precedent. Ezra Pound wrote haiku –
and in his early use of prayers as part of his poetry Eliot uses rhythms
that break, as these do.

> Eyes I dare not meet in dreams
> In death's dream kingdom
> These do not appear
>
> Between the idea
> And the reality
> Between the motion
> And the act
> Falls the Shadow
> For Thine is the Kingdom . . .
> For Thine is
> Life is
> For Thine is the . . .
>
> ('The Hollow Men')

Eliot's use of Christian prayer, and in *Ash Wednesday* of Dante, as
well as the canon of the mass, enables him to pause, and to be
repetitive, as a means of inducing meditative receptiveness. From the
Jesus Prayer of the Greek Orthodox Church, to the Buddhist 'Hail
the Jewel in the Lotus', such technique is becoming increasingly
familiar; eclectic traditions of prayer allow for much greater variation in the response of the reader, and Kathleen Raine, because she
does not adhere to a single tradition, has the advantage of finding her
own individual rhythms. This however is a lengthy process, and a
costly one.

Both 'Northumbrian Sequence' and *On A Deserted Shore* had
been prepared for by prose accounts of the personal events embodied
before what Edwin Muir termed the Fable, evolved out of the Story.[6]
His distinction is used at the opening of that volume of her autobiography in which she tells of her relationship with Maxwell:

> our deepest realizations, whether of knowledge or of love, are not our
> own inventions . . . during the enacting of this, the central event of my life,

I seemed to follow the form of an unfolding myth. (*The Lion's Mouth*, pp. 5–6)

The knowledge of Paradise must carry with it taste of exile, which Kathleen Raine had known from earliest childhood (see *Farewell Happy Fields*, p. 19), as in moments of anguish she knew divinity by the distance which separated her. ('Written in Exile', *Living in Time*, p. 19, is the first of many poems on this theme.) Another early poem describes the face imprinted on the Holy Shroud: 'That face, however closely we look, is always departing' ('The Holy Shroud', *The Year One*, p. 40).

This idea in her latest volume is applied to her human love, remembered as she watches the wild geese that Maxwell loved flying towards his boyhood home:

> You, like them, beyond sight
> Were always departing,
> I not the homecoming of your long flight.
> > (*The Oracle in the Heart*, p. 19)

Yet however different their vision, there was evidence of telepathy between them in their shared vision of the sleeper beneath the Rowan tree (*The Lion's Mouth*, p. 20):

> the double vision of a single mind
> Images from dream to dream within us travelled.
> > (*The Oracle in the Heart*, p. 19)

which absolved her from the charge of delusion, faced at the opening of *On A Deserted Shore*:

> Where my treasure is
> A grave:
> My heart also
> Empty.
> > Sorrow
> Is its own place, a glass
> Of memories and dreams; a pool
> Of tears. Narcissus pale
> Sees his own drowning face. (I)

Maxwell was buried in September 1969 under the Rowan tree that stood beside his shepherd's house at Sandaig, near Glenelg, the scene of the deserted shore. When he knew he was dying of cancer he sent for her, and said, 'In Spirit, accompany me.'

Kathleen Raine's four Edens had been Bavington, the Border hamlet in Northumberland where, during the First World War, she had lived with her aunt; Martindale, in Cumberland, where at the beginning of the Second World War she took her own children; this led to her friendship with Helen Sutherland and subsequent visits to Cockley Moor, near Penrith, Helen Sutherland's home. Here the 'Northumbrian Sequence' and many other poems were written, for Helen Sutherland became to her what Lady Gregory had been to her Master, Yeats. Finally, she was lent Maxwell's house at Sandaig where she stayed alone during his many journeys abroad or, in the year 1956–7, with the otter Mij whose tale is told both in *The Lion's Mouth* and in Maxwell's book which made him famous, *Ring of Bright Water* (1960).[7] The Hebrides, those supernatural Isles of the Blest, have been to many a symbol of a lost country that is met only in dreams. Encounter with the being who embodies the poet's vision establishes through that relationship a new relationship with everything else in creation; Dante's 'L'amor che muove il sole e l'altre stelle', to Wordsworth's 'Earth moved in one great presence of the spring'. Yet Platonic love, the theme of much of Yeats's best poetry, carries always the risk of total disruption.

And the Story, as distinct from the Fable? From the beginning, along with her sense of being exiled in the dreary London suburb where she was reared by a mother homesick for the Kielder of her own childhood, Kathleen Raine felt 'certain of identity' as a chosen one, set apart:

> an original and anterior dedication, one deep as life, a bond with my daimon not to be broken. No relation with any man has been for me of a comparable reality . . . As to the end to which I might be led, I more than half knew this could never be anything like marriage, nor even when it came to the point, a real love affair. For the end to which my love pointed was some absolute beyond this. I cared only for pure love – using the term as one might distinguish between 'pure' and 'applied' mathematics. (*The Land Unknown*, pp. 75, 115)

Maxwell, six years her junior, roused in her a feeling of occult power; to her he was a 'man of light', a scion of the Percies[8] of Northumberland, a reincarnation of childhood legends. The application of the same image to him and to the 'daimon' occurs more than once. It was after their meeting that she first 'found her range' as a poet in the poems of *The Year One*, as she herself records. The legend of Cupid and Psyche is used in the verses which Maxwell prefixed to *Ring of Bright Water* from her 'The Marriage of Psyche', which is an expansion of the earlier 'Psyche and the God'.

> In my love's house
> There are hills and pastures carpeted with flowers,
> His roof is the blue sky, his lamp the evening star . . .
> He has married me with a ring, a ring of bright water
> Whose ripples travel from the heart of the sea . . .
> He has married me with the sun's circle

Too dazzling to see, traced in a summer sky . . .
Transcendent touch of love summons my world to being.

Living encounter with a 'man of light', and the corresponding desire
to be a mirror to reflect truth and beauty to the beloved, follow the
assumption of a joint vision.

Gavin Maxwell never wrote another work to equal *Ring of Bright
Water*, but when he read Kathleen Raine's diaries the term he used
was 'outrageous'; he was moved immediately to compose his own
delightful acount of his own lost Paradise in *The House of Elrig*
(1965) – as the youngest of four children, surrounded by eccentric
but fascinating aunts and uncles, moving easily from one happy place
to another, he did not have to seek home in far away lands, which he
delighted to explore. There is wit and humour rather than intensity
here, and nothing of the sacred place. The book is an oblique denial,
the more powerful for having no direct reference whatsoever to the
experience that stimulated it.

After the death of the otter Mij, for which she felt guilty, Kathleen
could never resume the relationship as before. This little creature,
which Maxwell possessed for exactly a year and a day, completed the
vision of Paradise, though Mij, of course, does not come into the
poems, except in symbolic forms; here rather are wild birds of the
islands, bright flowers of the waterside. For Kathleen Raine's individual imaginative gifts included a natural inherited passion for
flowers – the first image she remembered being of a hollyhock by the
garden fence; while at Cambridge she had acquired the scientific
training of a botanist, with a broad base in general science. Without
effort, therefore, she can naturally recall an appropriate scientific
term, and include it in her verse without self-consciousness. Such
root words as 'sweet' grass, or 'bright' sea are joined with 'chromo-
some', 'stomata' or 'petiole'. One poem opens 'Sun/Flashed from
blades of salix, of chitin, of stone'.

The impulse to give and to serve was not incompatible with her
vocation, whilst it seemed that both served the same vision; but
whenever her own interpretation was offered, in her diary or in
narrative form, it repelled and angered Maxwell. Only after his death
could his image be projected poetically; as after her mother's death
also the image of her lost mother came into her poetry. The image of
a completed life, of an identity rounded and defined, has always
presented elegists with their theme. The great funeral sermons of a
Donne or a Bossuet poetically achieve this kind of definition in prose.

Kathleen Raine's first *Collected Poems* were dedicated to Maxwell
in 1956; but in her autobiography she withheld all description of him
because she felt too close to describe him. 'If I were to describe him,

as I can describe friends, less near, it would not be from that place from which I knew him.' (*The Lion's Mouth*, p. 18.) So he remains, like Adonais, to 'Beacon from the abode where the eternal are';[9] as in the heavenly landscape of 'sweet grass', flowers and shells, birds and butterflies, each in sacramental grace becomes the outward visible, the 'signature' of Mystery. 'Home' is a keyword in her poetry; one of her earlier poems in this volume where, as she explains, 'I found my range', is 'Spell to bring lost creatures home'. The spiritual home is that moment in which the whole of the universe is felt as a living organism, of which lover and beloved are cells or living parts; it was first directly experienced in a moment described in her autobiography (p. 119) as in Martindale she looked at a hyacinth. 'I could sense the very flow of life in the cells. I was not perceiving the flower but living it.' *The Hyacinth* appeared in her first volume in 1943, dedicated to her young son. (Had there been some unconscious memory also of Eliot's 'moment' in the hyacinth garden in the *Waste Land*?)

> Time opens in a flower of bells
> The mysteries of its hidden bed,
> The altar of the ageless cells
> Whose generation never have been dead.
>
> So flower angels from the holy head,
> So on the wand of darkness bright worlds hang.

Those bright worlds, the stars, were later to be used again and again for the image of separation between the divine and the time-bound. A poem on animals addressed to Maxwell preceded the arrival of Mij, the absolute and irreplacable symbolic child and angel of this spiritual union. In this poem, *The Victims*, finely observed detail is bound together by that kind of awed reverence in which a parent haloes a new born child:

> They walk towards us willingly and gently,
> Unblemished, the white kid, the calf,
> Their newborn coats scarce dry from the natal waters.

But even to look is to 'strike the first wound of sacrifice'. The ominous future of such innocence has been celebrated with a more direct biblical frame by her friend, Edwin Muir:

> They do not live in the world,
> Are not in time and space
> They are still without names; they have
> Never never turned back
> Into the memorial day.
> All is new and near
> In the unchanging Here

> Of the fifth great day of God
> That shall remain the same,
> Never shall pass away.
> On the sixth day we came.
>
> ('The Animals', *New Poems 1949–51*)

Love of this innocence is itself knowledge of exile; for the dedication to Maxwell of the *Collected Poems* (1956) Kathleen Raine used Milton's words of the lost Eden:

> with whom I share recollection of
> an Island salt and bare,
> The haunt of Seales and Orcs, and Seamews clang.

* * *

The urgent need which drove her from poetry into the history of poetry and scholarship was the need to justify her own vision as something more than projection, Narcissism. Had the final bitter knowledge of Maxwell's utter denial come at this time, she could hardly have survived (*The Lion's Mouth* p. 145). Now 'William Blake and the Neo-Platonists were still, in our separation of the regions of the imagination, incontestably my own, lending their dignity to my destitution' (ibid., p. 108). So she returned to Cambridge, and to the work on Blake which had already occupied her for some years (her little study in the series 'Writers and their Work' dates from 1951).

In returning to Cambridge, Kathleen Raine was, perhaps, facing an intellectual need to overcome the views implanted in her there as an undergraduate. When in 1926 she had come up as Exhibitioner in Natural Sciences from the prim and restricted suburbanism of Ilford where her father, a local schoolmaster, was a pillar of the Wesleyan Methodists, she had already been deeply wounded by the ferocious protectiveness with which he had broken up an entirely innocent and childish love affair with one of his own former pupils, who had introduced her to new fields of poetry and music. Cambridge gave at once liberation and yet became the ultimate place of exile. As the most beautiful woman of her time, she was pursued; a society of young men was formed merely to watch her pass in the street. I remember meeting one of them in the front court of Emmanuel, feebly gasping 'Gosh! Kathleen Raine!' She suffered from the sexual hunt; discarding with relief the Wesleyanism of her home, and swayed by the Major Scholar of her year, a Marxist from the Midlands, Kitty Karoline Klugmann, she adopted positivist views and turned from natural science (where she did well) to psychology; as a poet she assumed the 'sour new style' of anthropological eclecticism. Her condemnation of that Cambridge is at its severest in her study of another poet, Vernon Watkins, who left after one term.

> Tradition has more to give a poet than education has; and perhaps in the light of that tradition he divined the great lack in the Cambridge 'scientific' school of criticism of Richards Empson and (already) Leavis the denial of the imagination. I. A. Richards has since proved to be a Platonist, but the Cambridge trend, then and since, has been anti-imaginative, for the very good reason that Cambridge humanism is a by-product of the Cambridge scientific school of Russell and Wittgenstein. Years later Vernon Watkins wrote a ballad on Sodom and Gomorrah; but at the time he acted like Lot and left quickly a town past praying for. He was not deceived by the prestige of ignorance in high places. (*Defending Ancient Springs*, p. 61)

Kathleen Raine assumed the 'persona' in which she took pleasure of an emancipated agnostic. Her first poems appeared in the journal *Experiment*, with those of Empson and Bronowski. Two very forced essays on mythology, 'Atticus' and 'Hymn to B.V.M.', yet point with almost absurd intellectual assurance towards the two themes of the elegy for lost love and for the mother which were to be embodied fifty years later in mature verse. Her first lyric, based on one sung by Boris Ord's madrigal society, truly reflected the panics behind her assurance:

> 'Chloris when as I woo'.
> Pursuit, pursuit, pursuit!
> No, no, 'tis only discord round the frescoes and window latches!
> What is he thinking beneath that mask face?
> He pursues, pursues.
> Why, still deniest thou,
> Ah! why still deniest thou? . . .
> No, no, no, he never said it,
> He never said so!
> Does he know that my thoughts are crouching spider-like with
>   cold glittering eyes, lest he pursue?
> No, no, no, no, no, no.

Unpractised as they are, these lines transcribe the effect of Eliot's poetry and Tudor music upon the grounds of her natural fears. She renounced the Romantics on whom she had been bred – 'The rootless will always be attracted as I was towards the *avant-garde*' – but first she had suffered the scorn of Queenie Roth (who had put up some unwanted volumes of poetry for sale) when she chose Humbert Wolf, W. J. Turner and Vita Sackville-West's *The Land* (*The Land Unknown*, p. 39). She found Eliot for herself; who for her, as for all of us, was the poet of our time.

To retain the beauty of the Cambridge scene, and to escape Ilford where her father had found her a teaching post in a local school, she married, without love, Hugh Sykes, one of the editors of *Experiment*, whose verses seem almost a parody of her own:

> The much bitten
> tapesty
> holds
>   many
> moths
>
> (Sykes, 'Music in an Empty House')

Rescued by Charles Madge, she found herself, for the second time, living in someone else's dream 'noble though that dream was ... sooner or later the break must come – our love was rather a poetic fantasia than a marriage' (*The Land Unknown*, p. 93). Since she felt, like Ibsen's Nora, that her first duty was to herself rather than to husband or children, she slammed the door.

In the 1940s she intermittently joined the Roman Catholic Church; the poetry of that time, with its ecclesiastical symbols, was later discarded. An even more shadowy and unreal but erotic attachment to a young man, whom she loved only when he was *not* present, came at this nadir of her life; the story in many ways resembles that of another exile, Katherine Mansfield, who also recovered her Paradise in the wake of a bereavement – the loss of her younger brother in the First World War. Mansfield's Karori resembles Kathleen Raine's Eden.[10]

In returning to Cambridge, then, she was challenging what she had earlier absorbed. She met C. S. Lewis, Tom Henn and some congenial spirits among students in the place where her daughter and son had already followed their studies – Anna at Girton, James at Trinity. Though her main work was the preparation of *Blake and Tradition*, she taught a little, and roused in her students either devotion or terror; for she could be totally intransigent and did not temper the wind to the shorn lamb, academically speaking. In these years she established her own poetic line of tradition; Spenser, Milton, Blake, Wordsworth, Coleridge, Shelley, Yeats. Leavis disliked her work intensely. She and I went to Henn's Yeats Summer School in Sligo.

The knowledge of myth and symbol, the sacramental world, can to some extent be supported by Jungian psychology, though of those myths she particularly worked on, Cupid and Psyche, Demeter and Kore, and Narcissus, she found Jungian versions to be 'in the simple academic sense, incorrect' (*The Lion's Mouth*, p. 132). The Neo-Platonic learning which Blake acquired through many channels, but particularly the work of Thomas Taylor the Platonist, could be established in a scholarly way – and thus she was enabled, for instance, to read symbolism of the newly discovered Blake painting at Arlington Court, 'The Sea of Time and Space'; but metaphysics learnt from books is not what poets transmit. 'Knowledge of these symbols is essentially a kind of learning, but it is learning of the imagination, not merely of the conceptual mind' (*Defending Ancient Springs*, p. 13). Yet by now the great myths had lost their power:

> We know all myths but have none of our own . . . in such uncertainty we can be certain only of what to other periods seemed the least certain of all symbols, those of our own dreams and visions. These and not the cult have become the touchstone of truth (ibid., p. 138).

But since 'the sublime does not speak a private language' (Introduction to *Blake and Tradition*, p. xxvi) the poet must strive to bring life to symbols for those who do not consciously know them.

> Within tradition, poetry and the other arts have a clear function; to awaken in the reader or author the primordial images, and by this means to reintegrate the time-and-place bound ego with the eternal Self. (*The Inner Journey of the Poet*, 1982, p. 56).

She had pointed out that in the early poetry of Muir, the archetypes are insufficiently incarnated. Later he wedded them to history (*Defending Ancient Springs*, p. 5). The same is true of her own verses. In 'The Transit of the Gods' from *The Pythoness* (1949) mythology is both self-centred and yet realised from without; there is still too much intellectual assumption of a persona:

> Strange that the self's continuum should outlast
> The Virgin, Aphrodite and the Mourning Mother,
> All loves and griefs, successive deities
> That hold their kingdom in the human breast.
>
> Abandoned by the gods, woman with an ageing body
> That half remembers the Annunciation,
> The passion and the travail and the grief
> That wore the mask of my humanity . . .
>
> I, who have been Virgin and Aphrodite,
> The mourning Isis and the queen of corn,
> Wait for the last mummer, dread Persephone,
> To dance my dust at last into the tomb.

Yet in this same volume, in 'The Journey', addressed to Winifred Nicholson the painter (who also came from the Border Country), the mature poet speaks in the true voice that she was to recognise as her own in the following volume, *The Year One*. 'I would expect any profound revival of poetry to come from our exploration of the interior, the anterior landscape' Kathleen Raine was to observe still later (*The Land Unknown*, p. 138), 'The Journey' brings out the sense of an anterior history through a North Country landscape, in a manner that painters would certainly understand – such painters as John Piper or Winifred Nicholson herself. The image of the pilgrimage through many lives, as in 'The Transit of the Gods', is here fully incarnated (with memories of her own childhood in verses 2 and 5; in verse 6 of an earlier poem dedicated to her daughter, 'In the Beck'; and in verse 7 of another early poem, 'The Moment'):

> As I went over fossil hill
> I gathered up small jointed stones
> And I remembered the archaic sea
> Where once these pebbles were my bones . . .
> I was the trout that haunts the pool,
> The shadowy presence of the stream.
> Of many, many lives I leave
> The scattered bone and broken wing . . .
> Far I have come and far must go,
> In many graves my sorrow lies,
> But always from dead fingers grow
> Flowers that I bless with living eyes.

The 'small jointed stones' are old poems as well as old lives.

The rhythm of this poem compels assent; but the delicate precision of images could be supported by some of her earliest comments on Blake from the pamphlet of 1951:

It is often those who live between town and country, or for whom country scenes are a memory of childhood, a lost Eden, who have the keenest and most poignant sense of pastoral beauty . . . The imagination is for Blake, as for Coleridge, the divine presence in man, and his theory of the imagination is thus one that makes him, in the only significant sense, a religious artist . . . His vocabulary is simple as that of a child, and his symbols – roses, sun, flower, lion, lamb, beetle, and the little boy or girl – are few and universal (pp. 10, 25).

In Cambridge, working on Blake, Kathleen Raine recovered a basis for her own practice by devising an alternative to negative creeds with which she had rejected Ilford – 'it was like dissolving an iceberg', she said later, 'a piece of self-education'; whereas in 'Nativity', an early poem, she dreamt 'I have conceived a stone' (*LL*, p. 65). C. S. Lewis, who had himself written his version of Cupid and Psyche, *Till We Have Faces* (1956) appreciated both her poems and her Platonism. Perhaps a congenial scientist, such as Helen Megaw, acquainted with poetry, a designer of fine patterns from her crystallographic studies, might have supplied some soil for the roots. Willa and Edwin Muir came to live near by. But the final anguish of the relationship with Maxwell darkly dominated these years: to him she had surrendered the little Chelsea home which she had taken over from a friend of Helen Sutherland, the first London house which to her was 'home'. From this house he was to be married in 1960; near by they met briefly, in a moment that he records casually, and she poignantly in section 3 of 'Soliloquies upon Love' (*The Hollow Hill*, 1964):[11]

> Not hand in hand; I take that solitary way alone
> From the isle of orcs and seals and seamews' clang:
> But meeting long after, in a city street, my dear companion,
> It was as if the grave had opened and the light shone in.

She still kept her northern sacred places by visits to Cockley Moor until Helen Sutherland's death in 1965; then by visits to the Isle of Canna, the home of her friends the Campbells. She had meanwhile acquired another little house in the same Chelsea square, which she shared with Cecil Collins, the painter, and his wife; and after the death of Edwin Muir, with his widow, Willa.

But eventually she brought her parents from their retreat on the South Coast to receive a devoted care that in the end bound her to an enclosed life, and thus healed and re-established the relationship with her mother which was to provide themes for her poetry in the 1970s. Her intellectual work had satisfied the dreams of her father, but in the dreams of her mother she came eventually to recognise the endorsement of her own primal vision.

The *Collected Poems 1935–1980* are dedicated 'To my Mother, of whose unwritten poetry I have been inheritor, and sometimes I hope the author'. She had herself suffered as a mother from what she afterwards felt had been the exclusion of her children from her inner life, which had raised problems for them. She was a grandmother when she wrote 'I was the little girl of the one mother' ('Kore in Hades'). In *The Lost Country* (1971) she first began to bring ancestral figures from her own family into the verse of her sacred places. From 'Dream Flowers' she progresses to 'Heirloom', from Demeter and Persephone to a clear memory:

> She gave me childhood's flowers . . .
> Gave me her memories,
> But kept her last treasure:
> 'When I was a lass', she said,
> 'Sitting among the heather,
> Suddenly I saw
> that all the moor was alive!
> I have told no one before.'

Commenting on this, Kathleen Raine takes it as authentication of her own vision:

For certain kinds of knowledge (my mother's vision of the moor as 'alive', or my own hyacinth) once is enough. Those who have had the experience recognise instantly what is meant by others who speak of it; those who have not can never argue it away by logic or dissect it by science. (*The Lion's Mouth*, p. 12)

The plenitude of her own experience was sufficient: 'Life could give me no more, for there was nothing more I could ever need or want' (ibid., p. 110). A seven years' interval separated *The Hollow Hill* and *The Lost Country*; although the situation had been fully accepted years of work at the craft would still be needed before the word could be spoken. In those years of virtual seclusion with her widowed and aged mother, she was both mourning Gavin Maxwell's death and evolving her new form, condensing and concentrating her experience. The little garden at 47 Paulton's Square is the scene of a poem, dedicated to Willa Muir, about Edwin: 'The tree of night is spangled with a thousand stars' (*The Hollow Hill*, 1964). But, when the same scene is applied to her own loss, thirty lines are condensed into seven.[12] The gaps, the pauses, require time to mature, like wine that must be laid down.

> Night, Moon. Black leaves.
> I open the French windows wide:
> Between us other barriers,
> Invisible, infinite.
> On my threshold
> When my window is open on the night,
> Moths, black leaves, moonlight. (10. *On a Deserted Shore*)

The elegy was published four years after Maxwell's death, in the same year her mother died, aged ninety-three. The mother could be remembered in familiar ways, and into Kathleen Raine's poems of the 1970s come little domestic scenes, humour, tenderness, card-playing in Chelsea or at Canna House, her mother lying in the embryo's posture, light occasional verse for friends. The serenity of these latest poems emanates from a sacred landscape, a holy place that, in contrast to the violence of 'Northumberland Sequence' offers a second recognition of the eternal power entering human life.

Brevities of two series of 'Short Poems' in *The Oval Portrait* (1977) and *The Oracle in the Heart* (1980), meditations upon time, set aside even 'the harvest of learning I have reaped'.

> No written page more true
> Than blade of grass and drop of dew . . .
>
> No doctrine heart can heal
> As cloudless sky and lonely hill.

So in the last collection, dedicated to 'my daughter Anna':

> My sight with the clouds'
> Unimpeded rest in changing moves
> Across the sky; the aged in endless
> Unbecoming are at peace.

She even ventures to approach a new vision:

> Face of the presence; blue heaven, cloud,
> Mountain and wheeling bird:
> But only the pure in heart
> See God.
>
> ('Short Search for Truth', *Collected Poems*, p. 268)

and, 'In my Seventieth Year', to ask

> Is this perhaps what men called God
> Before the word lost meaning? this,
> That needs no doctrine to make plain,
> No cult to offer or withhold,
> A union more intimate
> Than breath of life, than flow of blood?
>
> ('The Oracle in the Heart', *Collected Poems*, p. 233)

The eternal moment, the moment of the hyacinth, may still recur, the sacred landscape confer assurance, as in the poem from the latest collection, 'Monessie Gorge':

> Seen from the train,
> Brown, brown water, swift
> Bubbles of foam, and as I pass, I am
> That stream, am one
> With the continuous, swept on
> My course, the pouring river
> In its shelving gorge for ever
> Wearing its rocks away.
>
> Live on in me, remembered ones,
> I am your future and your memory
> Who, within this ever moving now
> At rest in change, wore as I wear
> The seamless dress of earth and sea and sky . . .
>
> It crossed my mind
> That death might be like this
> Opening, this boundless going forth, to say
> 'this river is I', to extend
> Suddenly like air
> To be everywhere . . .
>
> Yet I had lost my situation in time and place
> And wondered, after,

> Who it was who had
> Been I when I said
> In fleeting joy 'I am the river.'
>
> (*Collected Poems*, pp. 242–3)

Yet she has also learnt the value of the negative landscape; in the Warton lecture of the British Academy, 1976, 'Waste Land – Holy Land', she defined what T. S. Eliot's desolate landscape, the landscape of exile, had achieved by its contraries; she compared it with Auden's purely social scene of desolation. This lecture is her most complete statement upon what as a poet she learnt from her early devotion to Eliot. (See *The Inner Journey of the Poet*)

She thinks her own language more accessible to the world than the traditional Christian language of T. S. Eliot or David Jones; yet *On a Deserted Shore* picks up echoes from St Teresa (44) the 20th Chapter of St John (15), the 24th chapter of St Luke (129), as well as Orpheus (4), Hans Andersen's Little Mermaid (59), and Southwell's Burning Babe (62); while in poems, like the late 'Wind' (*Collected Poems*, p. 224), the full resonance of the Christian symbol may be felt. Kathleen Raine does not deny that we are at the terminal point of Western civilisation, but she is turning from the formulations of the Neo-Platonists ('if you have to put in the name of Plotinus, you are really admitting defeat as a poet, because the poem should communicate without that' – a challenge to Yeats) and she now inclines towards the Psalms and the Hebrew prayer 'Praise be to Thee, King of the Universe, who createst Thy kingdom anew every morning': and to Blake's Jesus the Imagination, who said 'The kingdom of heaven is within you'; yet, 'we can't live entirely from within the psyche'.[13]

She can be curtly dismissive as ever of contemporary fashion – concrete poetry is 'just rubbish', the final expression of a materialist culture.

> I'm not concerned with the literary world. I don't see the literary world as something in itself. There is no such thing . . . poetry is only expressing the culture in which it is rooted. (*LL*, pp. 58, 61)

So that Leavis's idea of tradition is excluded – 'it could include the tradition that runs from Bacon to Newton to Locke to Darwin' and contain 'faslehood as well as truth' (ibid., p. 67).

Fifty years after the foundation of *Scrutiny* she came to share in her latest venture, the periodical *Temenos*, a form of witness to a much more scattered community. Among her friends are Greek Orthodox, Buddhists, Roman Catholics and Jews. Leavis's evasion of the final commitment may appear far from Kathleen Raine's knife-edge, which includes the poignancy of particulars, culminating in a

Blakean scene of ambiguity – fit for Empson, her earliest personal friend among the poets, to endorse.[14]

> 'Christmas Children'
> Little children running
> Each in a Paradise
> Within, as Eden was,
> Where invisible shine
> London's many coloured fairy lights
> Of Christmas trees from far
> Forests of night
> Sheltering home, father, mother,
> Puss, the koala bears,
> Tangerines, sugar mice, a star.
> Here and now boundless
> Their merriment.
>
> The dark hells walk past them unseen.

Elsewhere, tender mockery from her family when 'I call my grandson by my son's name' brings this new generation into the world of the hyacinth. She sees in son and grandson 'the one child returned from that place beyond time' and now it is her granddaughter who 'dreams undying dreams/And greets the high wind on the hills ('Too Many Memories', *The Oracle in the Heart*, p. 44). 'Home' is no longer the lost Paradise, but home in the familiar sense of the word; 'pure' and 'applied' love are reconciled.

Gradually, like a wild creature, domesticated – yet with the free places not forgotten – that sense of identity as the chosen one of which she had been so very sure when young appears to have been dissolved, in the 'endless unbecoming' of the old.

Chaucer, too, who had begun by defining what sounded like poetry, ends his definition with another word:

> The lyf so short, the craft so long to lerne,
> Th'assay so hard, so sharp the conquerynge,
> The dredful joy, always that slit so yerne:
> Al this I mene by Love
>
> (*The Parliament of Fowls*, 1–4)

Notes

1 A bibliography of her works – or rather a preliminary check-list – by Alan Clodd appeared in the *Ampleforth Journal* (Summer 1978, vol. LXXXIII, part II), and in the USA in a number of the Lindisfarne Letter (9, 1978) devoted to her work (Lindisfarne Press, W. Stockbridge, Mass.) referred to below as *LL*.

2 *LL*, p. 55. T. S. Eliot and Vernon Watkins both agreed that cadence could precede words. The significance of 'tunes running in the head' is familiar to all.

3 'The Mother of God' (*The Winding Stair*).

4 For the first see *The Lion's Mouth*, pp. 15–20. For the second, *Farewell Happy Fields*, pp. 55–7.

5 See Toyo Izutu. ('Haiku things and the haiku event', *Temenos*, 1.) In Noh drama the no-action (pauses) are the very essence of the performance and test of the actor's mastery, equivalent to a singer's holding a note.

6 *Faces of Day and Night*, originally prepared for publication in 1946, contains the germ of 'Northumbrian Sequence', written five years later. *The Lion's Mouth*, originally written in 1962, contains the germ of *On a Deserted Shore* (1973). Both prose versions were printed years after the poems had appeared.

7 *Ring of Bright Water* sold over a million copies, was made into a film, and was later adapted for children. His subsequent books, *The Rocks Remain* (1963), *The House of Elrig* (1965) and *Raven Seek Thy Brother* (1968) recount his own story. In the last he opens with the curse that Kathleen Raine uttered under the Rowan tree; a story she tells in *The Lion's Mouth* (pp. 72–4) in which she prayed that he might suffer as she was suffering for him.

8 Maxwell's mother was a daughter of the Duke of Northumberland, and though descent from the medieval Percies is indirect, the Maxwell line ran straight from the fifteenth century. His father was killed in the First World War, and he was brought up by his mother. He told Kathleen Raine of his homosexuality, but he had at least one mistress, and a brief, disastrous marriage.

9 See 'Star' (*The Hollow Hill*); 'Message to Gavin' (*The Lost Country*); *On a Deserted Shore*, prologue and passim; 'Short Poems' (*The Oval Portrait*); and 'Love Remembered' (*The Oracle in the Heart*).

10 See Andrew Gurr, *Writers in Exile* (Harvester, 1981), pp. 33–65 for a penetrating study of Katherine Mansfield. One of Kathleen Raine's Cambridge friends was Malcolm Lowry, whose idyll 'The Forest Path to the Spring', written many years later, has a close affinity of vision to the lost Paradise of the elegy. It, too, is elegaic. T. H. White, another of that group, shared her feeling for animals, but she did not possess the relative maturity of these two men who took what they needed from Cambridge. Their Romanticism survived. Both read English – Kathleen did not.

11 *Collected Poems*. In *The Lion's Mouth*, pp. 109–10, it felt 'like the sensation of an amputated limb'. Maxwell's mention is in *Raven Seek Thy Brother*.

12 In nothing does she resemble Yeats more than in her constant recasting and rewriting of the same material. Many of her discarded early poems read like rough sketches of later verse.

13 These quotations, like the one following, are taken from an interview made in 1979 and recorded in *LL*.

14 These verses are *not* included in *Collected Poems*.

X.

Notes on the Style of
Mrs Woolf

In reading any of the later novels of Mrs Woolf, a curious and persistent trick of style obtrudes itself on the attention: 'But for women, I thought, looking at the empty shelves, these difficulties are infinitely more formidable',[1] 'The mind is certainly a very mysterious organ, I reflected, drawing in my head from the window, about which practically nothing is known.'[2] 'There is a coherence in things, a stability: something, she meant, is immune from change and shines out (she glanced at the window with its ripple of reflected light). Here, she felt, putting down the spoon, here was the still space that lies about the heart of things.'[3]

The first two passages are ratiocinative, the last a description of a mood. Yet the little asides serve the same purpose in all three: by stressing time and place, they deflate the statement: the affirmation is given a relative value only: neither the reader nor the writer is implicated; they are not trapped into any admissions, or required to endorse anything in more than a qualified way. The effect has been described by T. E. Hulme:

> The classical poet never forgets the finiteness, the limit of man . . . If you say an extravagant thing, there is always the impression of yourself standing outside it and not quite believing it.

Mrs Woolf refuses to be pinned down in this way, and consequently she is debarred from a narrative technique, since this implies a schema of values, or even from the direct presentation of powerful feelings or major situations. In *Mrs Dalloway* the most powerful feelings depend on more powerful feelings long past: the old relationships between Clarissa, Peter, and Sally Seaton, the war experiences of Septimus Warren Smith. They are reflected, indirect, 'the reward of having cared for people.'[4] In *To the Lighthouse* the feelings are peripheral: they are minor manifestations of powerful forces, as, for instance, when Mrs Ramsay reassures her husband on the terrace. The success of the book is due to the fact that the reader accepts the implication of the major forces behind the small situations. But even then the real nature of the subject is cloaked by Mrs Woolf's method of description through a kind of metaphor which has a highly abstracting effect.

Whenever the direct presentation of powerful feelings or major situations is inescapable, Mrs Woolf takes refuge in an embarrassing kind of nervous irony (as in the bracketed passages in *To the Lighthouse*, part two).

> This violent kind of disillusionment is usually to be expected of young men in the prime of life, sound in wind and limb, who will later become fathers of families and directors of banks.[5]

> Here a girl for sale: there an old woman with only matches to offer.[6]

> A shell exploded. Twenty or thirty young men were blown up in France, among them Andrew Ramsay, whose death, mercifully, was instantaneous.

That 'mercifully' at least might have been spared.

For Doris Kilman and Charles Tansley (who are parallel figures) Mrs Woolf reserves her heaviest satire. Miss Kilman's feelings for Elizabeth or Tansley's sensations at the dinner party are analysed with a brutality that is faintly discomforting. They are both devoid of the social sense, scholars who have developed the intelligence at the expense of the arts of living.

The heroines on the contrary live by their social sense; they are peculiarly sensitive to tone and atmosphere; they are in fact artists in the social medium, with other people's temperaments and moods as their materials. Mrs Ramsay is the complement of Lily Briscoe,

> Mrs Ramsay, saying *Life stand still here:* Mrs Ramsay making of the moment something permanent (as in another sphere Lily herself tried to make of the moment something permanent) . . . In the midst of chaos there was shape: this eternal passing and flowing was struck into stability. *Life stand still here*, Mrs Ramsay said.[8]

It is the arresting of a single 'moment', a significant spot in the temporal sequence that is Art for Mrs Ramsay and Mrs Woolf. In *The Spot on the Wall*, Mrs Woolf describes her technique, which is essentially static. A single moment is isolated and forms a unit for the sensibility to work on. The difficulty lies in relating the various moments. Intensity is the only criterion of a detached experience and there is a consequent tendency for everything to be equally intense in Mrs Woolf's works. Everything receives the same slightly strained attention: the effect is not unlike that of tempera painting, where there is exquisite delicacy of colour, but no light and shade. (The connection of this with the refusal to assent to a statement absolutely is too obvious to need any stressing.)

Mrs Woolf's difficulties have always been structural. In *Jacob's Room* she hardly attempted a solution: in *Mrs Dalloway* she began the rigid telescoping of the time sequence which was developed in *To the Lighthouse*. A series of echoes and cross references form the real framework of the book; they are of the kind Joyce had used in *Ulysses*, but there is nothing to correspond to the more bony support which in *Ulysses* is provided by the structure of the episodes. The precarious stability of *To the Lighthouse* dissolved into the muddle of *Orlando* (in any case a *jeu d'esprit*), and the futile counterpointing of *The Waves*.

Mrs Woolf's books seem to be built up in a mosaic from the 'moments': scenes, descriptions, odd names recur from time to time. Here is a typical case:

> Already the convolvulus moth was spinning over the flowers. Orange and purple, nasturtium and cherry pie, were washed into the twilight but the tobacco plant and the passion flower over which the great moths spun were white as china.[9]

> How she loved the grey white moths spinning in and out, over the cherry pie, over the evening primroses.[10]

Moll Pratt the flowerseller and the Reverend Edward Whittaker, figures who appear for a moment only, are in *Jacob's Room* and *Mrs Dalloway*; and the Dalloways themselves are of course from *The Voyage Out*.

This kind of thing developed in the subtler correspondence between parts one and three of *To the Lighthouse*, as for instance, Cam's recollections of the stag's head.[11]

The significant moments, the units of Mrs Woolf's style are either delicate records of the external scene, expressed in epigrammatic metaphor usually ('The whole platefuls of blue sea', 'The dragonfly paused and then shot its blue stitch further through the air') or the presentation of a mood such as Mrs Ramsay's reverie on the terrace.[12] These moods are hardly ever dramatic i.e., bound by the limitations of the character who experiences them. The personality of Mrs Ramsay on the terrace or of Mrs Dalloway in her drawing-room does not matter: neither their individuality nor the plot is of any relevance. The mood is in fact an isolated piece of pure recording, of a more complex kind but not essentially different from the epigrammatic metaphor. It is less an emotion than a sensation that is presented: the feeling is further depersonalised by Mrs Woolf's use of metaphor: for instance in the description of Mr Ramsay appealing to his wife.[13]

These two elements of Mrs Woolf's style, the observation of the external world and the description of moods, are separated out in her last book, *The Waves*. The inter-chapters describe the movements of sun and tides (the sea is for Mrs Woolf a symbol of the eternal and indifferent natural forces):[14] this movement forms a kind of parallel to the development of the lives of the characters. But the effect of a page or two of epigrammatic metaphor is very fatiguing: the myopic observation, the lack of variations in the tension impose a strain on the reader. Sometimes phrase-making conquers accuracy: 'the lark peeled his clear ring of song and dropped it through the silent air' suggests the long call of a blackbird, but hardly the trills and twitters of the lark.

In the main portion of the book there are no solid characters, no clearly defined situations and no structure of feelings: merely sensation in the void. Without any connections of a vital sort between them, with no plot in the Aristotelian sense, the sensations are not interesting. Emotions are reduced to a description of their physical accompaniments: the attention is wholly peripheral. This for example is the equivalent of the experience of being in love:

> Then there is the being drawn out, eviscerated, spun like a spider's web, twisted in agony round a thorn: then a thunder clap of complete indifference: the light blown out: then the return of measureless inexpressible joy: certain fields seemed to glow green for ever.[15]

There had been hints of this danger even in the earlier works: 'how could one express in words these emotions of the body? To want and not to have, sent up all her body a hardness, a hollowness, a strain.'[16] Physical sensations, which are immediately present, and have no relations to any schema of values, are all that Mrs Woolf dares to assume in her readers.

All attempt to order and select has gone.

> There is nothing that one can fish up with a spoon, nothing that one can call an event . . . How impossible to order them rightly, to detach one separately or give the effect of the whole . . . Nevertheless, life is pleasant, life is tolerable. Monday is followed by Tuesday, then comes Wednesday.[17]

Mrs Woolf never, as is so frequently asserted, attempts to reproduce the process of thinking. Such generalised activity does not interest her: moreover, thinking implies a thesis which one is ready to defend. Mr Ramsay, who is a philosopher, 'thinks' with the most helpless particularity: the progress of human thought is symbolised for him by an alphabet, just as for Lily Briscoe, a large kitchen table stands for the mental pursuits of Mr Ramsay himself. Their mental atmospheres are indistinguishable: and in both cases, the mood is not one of thought but of reverie.

The heroines are astonishingly ingenuous. Their tact and sensitiveness are preserved in a kind of intellectual vacuum. Mrs Dalloway 'muddled Armenians and Turks: and to this day, ask her what the Equator was and she did not know.'[18] Mrs Ramsay ponders 'A square root? What was that? Her sons knew. She leant on them: on cubes and square roots: that was what they were talking about . . . and the French system of land tenure . . . She let it uphold her, this admirable fabric of the masculine intelligence.'[19] Compare the dependence of Mrs Flanders and even of Lady Bruton.

The camouflage in *A Room of One's Own* serves the same purpose as this nervous particularising: it prevents Mrs Woolf from committing the indelicacy of putting a case or the possibility of her being accused of waving any kind of banner. The arguments are clearly serious and personal and yet they are dramatised and surrounded with all sorts of disguises to avoid an appearance of argument.

The shrinking of the heroines is too conscious as the playfulness of *A Room of One's Own* is too laboured. To demand 'thinking' from Mrs Woolf is clearly illegitimate: but such a deliberate repudiation of it and such a smoke screen of feminine charm is surely to be deprecated. Mrs Woolf has preserved her extraordinary fineness and delicacy of perception at the cost of some cerebral etiolation.

Notes

1 *A Room of One's Own*, p. 79.
2 ibid., p. 146.
3 *To the Lighthouse*, p. 164.
4 *Mrs Dalloway*, p. 13.
5 *Jacob's Room*, p. 247.
6 ibid., p. 132.
7 *To The Lighthouse*, p. 207.
8 ibid., p. 249.
9 *Jacob's Room*, p. 90.
10 *Mrs Dalloway*, p. 22.
11 *To the Lighthouse*, pp. 177, 313.
12 ibid., pp. 29–30.
13 ibid. p. 61.
14 *Mrs Dalloway*, p. 61; *To the Lighthouse*, p. 30.
15 *The Waves*, p. 274.
16 *To the Lighthouse*, pp. 274–5.

17 *The Waves*, pp. 280–2. Cf. *Monday or Tuesday*, her first attack on the problem of the time sequence.

18 *Mrs Dalloway*, p. 185.

19 *To the Lighthouse*, p. 164.

Mrs Woolf's reactions to this article are recorded in *The Diary of Virginia Woolf*, ed. Anne Olivier Bell, vol. iv 1931–5 (1982) pp. 100–101.

What [should be] is the right attitude towards criticism? What ought I to feel & say & do when Miss B. devotes an article in Scrutiny to attacking me? She is young, Cambridge, ardent. And she says I'm a very bad writer. Now I think the thing to do is to note the pith of what is said—that I dont think—then to use the little kick of energy which opposition supplies to be more vigorously oneself. It is perhaps true that my reputation will now decline. I shall be laughed at & pointed at. What should be my attitude—clearly Arnold Bennett & Wells took the criticism of their youngsters in the wrong way. The right way is not to resent; not to . . . be long suffering & Christian & submissive either. Of course, with my odd mixture of extreme rashness & modesty (to analyse roughly) I very soon recover from praise & blame. But I want to find out an attitude. The most important thing is not to think very much about oneself. To investigate candidly the charge; but not fussily, not very anxiously. On no account to retaliate by going to the other extreme—thinking too much. And now that thorn is out—perhaps too easily but then of course John interrupted.

XI.

To the Lighthouse[1]

There is a general agreement that *To the Lighthouse*, Virginia Woolf's fifth novel, is also her best. She herself thought so, and twice recorded that best of all was the dinner party, the climax of part I (*Letters*, ed. N. Nicolson, iii, 373, 383).

Its first title was *The Old Man* but it is in the figure of Mrs Ramsay, rather than her husband's, that Mrs Woolf's technique (it had already been called impressionist) flowered in a blend of sensation, reverie, terror, intuition and sympathy, caught in the flying moments of one late September afternoon and evening of about 1910.

Mr and Mrs Ramsay are generally agreed to have been modelled on Virginia Woolf's parents, Leslie and Julia Stephen; even before she had finished it, the author embarked on a fantastic biography of her friend Vita Sackville-West, who in *Orlando* is superimposed on portraits of her ancestors. The autobiographical element, therefore, in *To the Lighthouse* should not be simplified or taken out of context; neither the characters nor the scene are transcriptions of any one person or place. Before she wrote it, Mrs Woolf had already written *Mr Bennett and Mrs Brown*, putting her objections to the superficial realism of the Edwardian novelists Galsworthy, Bennett and Wells; setting against them the new novel of character, in Lawrence, Joyce and Forster. To these may be added Proust, whose influence was deeply felt in the early twenties in England; and the minor talent of Katherine Mansfield. Her novella 'Prelude', with less depth of characterisation, forecasts the mood and setting of part I of *To the Lighthouse*, evoking a far-off Eden, a demi-Paradise, which Mrs Woolf set in the Hebrides, where the Ramsays have a holiday house. Their eight children and six guests complete the cast – the last include a distinguished botanist, an unsuccessful poet who has taken to drugs, a woman painter, an aggressive graduate student, a young couple who in the course of the day become engaged. Their merging and diverging moods vibrate across each other's sensibilities in a lattice of human relationships.

The poetic threnody, *Time Passes*, which constitutes part II, brings up as dominant the rhythms not of human relationships but of natural growth and decay, of life and death. The seasons turn and return in their courses, lights flicker over the deserted and decaying house, whilst in short parentheses, almost like telegrams in their curtness, the effect on the human group is registered – death, marriage, more deaths.

According to Mrs Woolf, this part 'gave me more trouble than all the rest of the book put together' (*Letters*, iii, 374); but its method was to form the basis of her next novel, *The Waves*.

In part III, which is briefer, harsher, more analytic than part I, some of the survivors return, and echoes of part I repeat themselves like *leit-motifs* in a Wagnerian opera. The sea journey to the lighthouse, denied the eager small boy in part I, is accomplished; the picture of the house and Mrs Ramsay is finished, both achievements being counter-pointed against each other, as attention shifts from the boat cutting its way towards the lighthouse, to Lily Briscoe at her easel with the poet beside her. Mrs Ramsay and two of the elder children are dead; a kind but ineffectual old lady who is added to the group only emphasises the gap. Their father takes the two younger children, who do not want to visit the lighthouse, in a ritual of mourning and satisfaction for what had earlier been denied. For mourning is an arbitrary emotion, and Lily Briscoe who at one point feels no grief at all, suddenly finds herself weeping and calling aloud, 'Mrs Ramsay! Mrs Ramsay!' (p. 209).

'To want and not to have, sent up all her body a hardness, a hollowness, a strain' (pp. 206–7). Life and death, light and darkness are the polarities of the novel; interpretation also has to swing between the two extremes of autobiography and symbolism. Mrs Woolf subscribed to neither; her nephew's *Life* (1972) and the new edition of her *Letters* offer her own direct comments on both.

When in 1878 Leslie Stephen married Julia Duckworth, each had been widowed. Leslie Stephen's one child, Laura, was hopelessly retarded; Mrs Duckworth's trio included the beautiful Stella, who, like Prue Ramsay, was to die shortly after her marriage, and two sons. The four young Stephens were a decade or more junior to the Duckworths, but the total of the combined group was eight (the number of the Ramsays). Their holiday home, Talland House, outside St Ives, Cornwall, faced the Godrevy lighthouse; this little town was already a haunt of painters. As her father's family was Scots, Mrs Woolf moved the scene to the Hebrides, although indignant Scots pointed out that dahlias, rooks, elms and carnations are

not found there. 'Dear me, what's to be done about it?' was her
insouciant comment, but to an old friend she observed: 'People in the
Hebrides are very angry. Is it Cornwall? I'm not so sure as you are'
(*Letters*, iii, 388). Of course it is no one place: but in times of distress
Mrs Woolf always returned to Cornwall for comfort.

> The only Paradise, Proust said,
> Is the lost country that has passed
> Out of time and into mind.

Memories of 1890 have been moved twenty years on.

The salient characteristics of Mr Ramsay depend on Leslie
Stephen's powerful, attractive and exasperating character. Mrs
Woolf had already made a first sketch of her parents in Mr and Mrs
Ambrose of *The Voyage Out*. Leslie Stephen, one of the leading
figures of the literary world, editor of the *Dictionary of National
Biography*, had become like that other great Scottish editor, James
Murray of the *New English Dictionary*, something of a domestic
tyrant to his large family. His irrational fear of poverty was such that
some friends once planned a subscription to save him from ruin, only
to discover that he was nowhere near ruined. Mrs Ramsay's recur-
rent fear – 'The bill for the greenhouse would be fifty pounds' –
represents faintly the effect of the cries, heard weekly by the
Stephens, that all were bound for the workhouse.

Mr Ramsay's fine scholarship, his integrity, his sense of justice, his
concern for suffering compete with his ravenous need for sympathy
and reassurance, which is satisfied by the devotion of his wife. In part
III, when Lily Briscoe tries to console him, all she can think of is to
praise his beautiful boots. It is enough however; for Mr Ramsay was
very proud of his specially made boots and could talk of them for
hours. The children resent these demands, they resent his display of
grief, they band against his tyranny.

Mrs Ramsay evoked from Mrs Woolf's sister, Vanessa Bell,
immediate recognition:

> . . . in the first part of the book you have given a portrait of mother which
> is more like her than anything I could have conceived of as possible. It is
> almost painful to have her so raised from the dead. You have made me feel
> the extraordinary beauty of her character, which must be the most
> difficult thing in the world to do. You have given father I think as clearly,
> but perhaps I may be wrong, that isn't so difficult. There is more to catch
> hold . . . As far as portrait painting is concerned, you seem to me a
> supreme artist . . . then of course there is the relationship between the two,
> which perhaps is more your subject . . . I know that in spite of all my
> personal interest I shouldn't have been moved, if it hadn't moved me
> impersonally too. (*Letters*, iii, 572–3.)

Vanessa Bell, herself a painter, had enjoyed the closest confidence of Virginia from childhood. The author replied:

> I'm in a terrible state of pleasure that you should think Mrs Ramsay so like mother. At the same time, it's a psychological mystery why she should be; how a child could know about her; except that she has always haunted me . . . Probably there is a great deal of you in Mrs Ramsay; though in fact, I think you and mother are very different in my mind. (*Letters*, iii, 383.)

Julia Stephen, who died in 1895 when Virginia was thirteen, had been named for her aunt, the photographic artist, Julia Cameron, and like many of the family, was famous for her Pre-Raphaelite type of beauty; her own sense of design lay in the ordering of human relationships. Mrs Ramsay's art is first shewn in the scene where she calms her husband as she sits at the window with her youngest boy (p. 43), till the man, 'filled with her words, like a child who drops off satisfied', said with humble gratitude, restored and renewed, that he would take a turn; he would watch the children playing cricket.

James, standing between her knees, feels the virtue she expends; he resents his father's demands. In this scene, Mrs Ramsay is indeed goddess-like; she has not only the charisma of a woman like E. M. Forster's Mrs Moore (in *A Passage to India*) but the impersonal life of the great fountain in a poem like Yeats's *Ancestral Houses*.

> Life overflows without ambitious pains
> And rains down life until the basin spills . . .

Yet she is also the lady of the house, attending to many duties at once, consoling both son and husband, knitting her stocking for the lighthouse keeper's son, posing for the painter, dreaming her own reverie to the sound of waves – which, usually calming, suddenly thundered in her ears when the men stopped talking, warning her that her husband might need attention.

Mr Ramsay says they cannot go to the lighthouse because the weather signs are bad; with a fine disregard for facts Mrs Ramsay tries to avert the blow to her little son. Facts are not her province, except when they relate to the practical well-being of those she cherishes.[2]

She plans the lives of others rather ruthlessly. Paul Rayley and Minta Doyle are to marry; marry they do, not very happily. Lily Briscoe recognises, under Mrs Ramsay's pressure, that she doesn't want to marry anyone, when 'Paul Rayley turned on her cheek the heat of love, its horror, its cruelty, its unscrupulosity. It scorched her, and Lily, looking at Minta . . . flinched for her, exposed to those fangs' (p. 119).

As she presides over her magnificent dish of *boeuf en daube*, everyone is a little in love with Mrs Ramsay. In response to an agonised signal from her hostess, Lily bestirs herself to be pleasant to the aggressive young graduate, whose life is soured by his 'ambitious pains', as he arrogantly insists on his difference from this privileged group.

The merging and melting of all differences in a feeling of well-being, and in the beauty of the dish of fruit – arranged by one of the younger girls – culminates when the children burst into little spurts of laughter against the absurdity of some of their mother's pet opinions. Her husband joins in. It is the laughter of security and love; it shines like fire.

So, for the symbolists, Mrs Ramsay is Rhea, she is Demeter, she is herself a symbol. Modern critics can produce such alarming comments as:

> A discussion of the androgynous nature of the Lighthouse symbol does not reveal its full meaning, for it is also associated with ideas about time, death and egoism.[3]

If Charles Tansley – who was writing a dissertation 'about the influence of somebody on something' – had come out of the book to comment on it, the original object would have offered him many possibilities. But in a letter to Roger Fry, Mrs Woolf disclaimed these readings:

> I meant *nothing* by the Lighthouse. One has to have a central line down the middle of the book to hold the design together. I see that all sorts of feelings would accrue to this, but I refused to think them out and trusted that people would make it the deposit for their own emotions, which they have done, one thinking it means one thing, one another. I can't manage symbolism except in this vague, generalized way. Whether its right or wrong, I don't know, but directly I'm told what a thing means, it becomes hateful to me. (*Letters*, iii, 385.)

The steady beam of the lighthouse means so much but so vaguely to Mrs Ramsay who thinks the third long steady stroke of the beam is peculiarly 'her' stroke (p. 73). The three strokes of the lighthouse beam – light, darkness, light – are repeated in the design of the book itself with its three parts.

When in part III, the party reaches the lighthouse, it presents to them that gaunt, shabby look, 'glaring black and white', encrusted with weeds, stained with the sea, that always repels when a sea-girt lighthouse is actually approached. Mr Ramsay had been reciting to himself Cowper's *Castaway* – 'We perished, each alone' – and James, seeing 'a stark tower on a bare rock' was confirmed in some obscure feeling about his own character (p. 236). The metaphors of part I are brought to life; Mr Ramsay, wrestling with his thoughts, had called on qualities that would have sustained the leader of a desperate Polar expedition (pp. 39–40); in part III he does lead a party, leaping ashore at last like a young man, having won over his son, with his sudden praise, 'Well done!' for 'steering like a born sailor' (p. 239). In part I, Cam, the youngest girl, had been frightened by the shadows cast from the skull of a wild boar hung in her room, but Mrs Ramsay had draped it with her shawl, soothing Cam with a tale of how the fairies now would love it; it was like a bird's nest; it was like a beautiful mountain . . . and in the boat, as Cam falls half asleep, the images return to her, consoling, part of herself, though she has forgotten their origins. For the artist, painting her picture, mourning Mrs Ramsay, some shade miraculously reappears at the window. She draws a line in the centre of the picture completing the design.

Simultaneously the party land. 'He must have reached it,' said Lily Briscoe. It is finished, she said to the old poet dreaming beside her, who, after Andrew Ramsay's death in the war – he had loved Andrew – wrote deeper poetry.

In part II we have learnt in asides of the 'rather sudden' death of Mrs Ramsay, of Prue's marriage and her death a few months later, of Andrew being blown up with twenty or thirty young men in France. These asides, coupled with banal expressions of conventional grief, and with the animal-like ramblings of an old caretaker, break in to the delicate web of the passing time, savagely and not really success-fully. Mrs Ramsay knew that life could betray all trust; but the writer does not wish to show this aspect of things.

The effect of cant phrases and of Mrs McNab may be intended to work like the clown's jests in a scene of Elizabethan tragedy, but the fusion does not occur. The inner weather, reflected in part I now from one member of the party, now from another, is basically temperate; in part III the *effects* of death are shown, but the storm is past.

Mrs Woolf herself had mourned the early death of her brother Thoby in 1906; Andrew Ramsay the young mathematician suggests also Frank Ramsay, greatest mathematician of his generation, who died young just after the book was written; suggests too, of course, something of those deaths in the First World War, which had cast a lengthier shadow in the previous novel, *Mrs Dalloway*, in the suicide of the shell-shocked Septimus. Jacob, the hero of an earlier novel, *Jacob's Room*, had also died in war; the sheep's skull as an emblem in this other early work looks forward to the boar's skull in *To the Lighthouse*.

The evocation of the past, like the beautifully blended culinary masterpiece which is the triumph of part I, is complete in this first part. Parts II and III add perspective, as the ease and intuitive shaping give way to a more conscious craftsmanship.

... so much depends, she thought, upon distance; whether people are near us or far from us; for her feeling for Mr Ramsay changed as he sailed further and further across the bay (pp. 221–2).

The comedy of *To the Lighthouse*, which is the comedy of affection, plays over all except Charles Tansley who is last recalled (he does not appear in part III) preaching in tones of hate the brotherhood of man.

* * *

The book was written with unusual speed; begun in mid-June 1925, part I was finished by April 1926; 'Time Passes' was composed during the turbulence of the General Strike in May 1926; by November Mrs Woolf was revising, by January the typescript was ready, and it was published on 5 May 1927.

In her own life, Mrs Woolf lived with experiences which she did not choose to make part of any book. When she was thirteen and very soon after her mother died, she suffered her first mental collapse and made an attempt at suicide. The rasping note with which the horrors are dismissed in this story becomes more explicable, together with the limitation to what the American poet Conrad Aiken termed 'a delicious parochialism' in the cultivated, sensitive and privileged life of good taste. The world of privilege to which Virginia Woolf was born was by 1927 already far in the past; but the vision at the centre is, in the words of another friend and contemporary, T. S. Eliot, 'quick now, here now, always'.

Notes

1 This chapter was originally published as the Introduction to the Everyman edition (1978) of *To the Lighthouse*.
2 See above for an example of the encounter between Mr and Mrs Ramsay, and her attempt to protect her little son from disappointment, p. 84.
3 *To the Lighthouse, a Casebook*, p. 194.

Acknowledgements

The following articles in this volume were originally published elsewhere, and I am grateful for permission to include them in this collection, and would like to express thanks to all concerned: 'Living the Gothic Pastoral Romance', originally published as 'The Elegant Eccentrics', *The Modern Language Review*, vol. XLIV, no. 2, April 1949; 'My Cambridge', in *My Cambridge*, ed. R. Hayman 1977; 'Queenie Leavis: The Dynamics of Rejection', *The Cambridge Review*, November 1981; 'Notes on the Style of Mrs Woolf', *Scrutiny*, vol. I, no. 1, May 1932; '*To the Lighthouse*', the Introduction to the Everyman edition of that novel, 1978.

The following papers were originally presented as lectures: 'Reticence in the Later Novels of Jane Austen', to graduates of Girton College, Cambridge, 1976; 'Barbara Bodichon, George Eliot and the Limits of Feminism', The Bryce Memorial Lecture, Somerville College, Oxford, 1975; 'Paris in the Bernhardt Era', Guelph University, Ontario, 1977; '*A Doll's House*: The Unweaving of the Web', and 'In Dreams begin Responsibilities' are adapted from lectures given for the Cambridge English Tripos.

Quotations for Ibsen are taken from the Oxford Ibsen, ed. J. W. McFarlane and for Strindberg from the translation of Strindberg by Michael Meyer (Secker and Warburg).

I am grateful to Mrs. P. C. Rignold for help in the preparation of this volume and to the editorial staff of the Harvester Press, especially Sue Roe, for their kind assistance.